P9-DGH-651

FAST & FLAVORFUL PALEO COOKING

⤜ Dedication ⤛

I dedicate this book to my mother, Pamela, who always wanted me to use my education to help others. I wish you were here to see this book and all that I have accomplished with my website. You would be so proud.

And to everyone who has ever been in my shoes and felt utterly abandoned and dismissed by conventional medicine, or been given a hopeless outlook and told there is nothing you can do to improve, and that you're foolish for thinking a change in diet will have any positive impact. You're not crazy. It's not all in your head. You deserve better. And eating whole, unprocessed food absolutely can make a huge positive impact in how you feel. This book is here to support you on your journey to better health, making sure every bite along the way is delicious.

CONTENTS

Introduction

Thank you so much for picking up a copy of this cookbook. If you don't know me yet, my name is Amanda Torres, and I am the founder of the popular website The Curious Coconut (www.thecuriouscoconut.com), a trusted source for delicious and creative gluten-free, dairy-free, allergy-friendly food suitable for the Paleo diet as well as the autoimmune protocol (AIP), plus evidence-based health and wellness articles.

Since founding my website in 2012, I've been able to reach millions of people all over the world. I also regularly do events locally in Memphis, Tennessee, featuring my first cookbook *Latin American Paleo Cooking*. I've had countless conversations about my health story and the Paleo diet with people who are searching for a way to feel better. And one of the most common hurdles people tell me about when it comes to changing their diet is lack of time to cook meals.

That's exactly why I wrote this book.

Cooking fresh, delicious, anti-inflammatory food doesn't have to take hours and hours in the kitchen. It doesn't have to mean you can only cook on the weekends and reheat leftovers every night. No, you can cook from fresh on a busy weeknight and make a flavorful dish the whole family will love to eat. And you can do it right on your stovetop and in your oven, no fancy or expensive cooking appliances needed.

While "replacement" recipes for things like breads and cakes and the like can certainly make Paleo more fun, they can be a distraction from the core of the lifestyle: high-quality proteins and a large variety of colorful plants. Plus, replacement recipes can take a lot of time and effort to prepare. This book focuses on delicious, staple proteins and vegetables that have been my go-to recipes over the years. This book is almost flourless and doesn't require any hard-to-find specialty Paleo-specific ingredients.

I've been able to adhere to Paleo and even the AIP while working a high-paced research job demanding 60-plus hours a week from me, so I know you can do it too with the help of this book.

My Story:
Discovering Food as Medicine

My professional background is as a neuroscientist. I worked in biomedical research for more than a decade, studying everything from the long-lasting effects of early life trauma on anxiety and memory, to the endocannabinoid system, to using bone marrow-derived stem cells to treat the brain after a stroke. While I absolutely loved working in research, the demanding hours, stressful work environment and exposure to toxic chemicals was too much for my body.

My health decline began in grad school in 2007. I became obese, developed the debilitating autoinflammatory skin condition hidradenitis suppurativa (HS), had IBS-D, hypertension, metabolic syndrome, pre-diabetes, depression and insomnia. I always used all of my sick days at work, and I took a dozen different medications every day just to get by.

But I wanted more than to just "get by." I was only in my early twenties and knew there had to be a way to feel better. Western medicine and conventional advice utterly failed me and only offered a bleak outlook of needing more medications over time and only getting worse, not better. But I refused to accept powerlessness over my body and searched for answers. Then in 2010, I stumbled upon the Paleo diet.

I felt better within days. It was as if a switch had been flipped to "off" for the IBS-D. My head was clearer, my energy increased, my mood improved, my sleep improved and I lost a ton of inflammation weight very quickly: 10 pounds (4.5 kg) and 2 inches (5 cm) off my waist (a lot of that was bloating!) in the first 2 weeks.

Over the course of that first year, I would go on to lose 80 pounds (36 kg). I have maintained this weight loss to date, and put all of my health ailments into remission, including the HS.

Multiple dermatologists had told me I would be on antibiotics for life because of the HS and that eventually I would need disfiguring surgeries to "manage" it, so I am incredibly grateful that I am able to keep it in remission with my diet and lifestyle choices.

Food can truly be our medicine, and going Paleo taught me that gluten (the protein found in wheat, barley and rye) was making me sick, inflamed and obese.

I've also found tremendous healing from Chinese medicine and have gotten acupuncture at least once a week since 2014, and I never plan to stop. While I no longer take any medications, I do utilize supplements to support my health and take custom blended Chinese herbs from my acupuncturist.

I am so honored to be able to aid you on your own healing journey with this book and through my website. I can't wait to hear what you think when you cook these dishes!

Amanda

P.S. Use this QR code to navigate to a resources page dedicated to this book on my website. It will always be updated with information about specific tools or ingredients as well as with any notes or clarifications. You can also leave comments and ask questions there if you run into any issues while cooking through this book.

How to Use This Book

This book is organized by how fast the recipes in each chapter will be on your table, with recipes ready in 15 minutes or less appearing at the beginning of each chapter, 30 minutes or less in the middle and recipes ready in 45 minutes or less closing out each chapter.

Additionally, I have prepared a couple of visual charts to help you. The Side Dish Finder (page 174) allows you to see at a glance which side dishes will pair perfectly with the protein you're cooking based on cooking method and time, so that you can make complete meals with ease.

The Batch Cooking Baking Guide (page 176) shows you which dishes cook at the same temperature and for the same amount of time in the oven, so that you can make two recipes at once and cook ahead.

Lastly, the Partially Used Fresh Ingredients Guide (page 178) shows you which recipes use partial fresh ingredients, like cans of coconut milk, bunches of fresh herbs, etc. so that you can know which recipes to cook within a few days of each other in order to not let any of your ingredients accidentally go to waste.

One more important thing to know about this book: The instructions are written for stainless steel cookware. If you need pointers on how to cook like a pro with your stainless steel cookware, check out page 173.

CHICKEN, TURKEY AND EGGS

For weeknight-friendly chicken dishes, you need to work with individual cuts of chicken, like the breasts, thighs, drumsticks, wings and even ground chicken. I know that for some, chicken can be intimidating because it can be bland and rubbery when cooked improperly. Don't worry: after cooking the recipes in this book, you'll be skilled at turning all of these cuts into tender, juicy, delicious main dishes that your whole family will gobble up. Speaking of gobbling, the only turkey you'll find here is ground turkey, which is the only kind that's quick enough to cook up on a busy evening. And the egg dishes are not just great for breakfast, but for any meal.

← See recipe on page 26.

Persian Herb Frittata (Kuku Sabzi)

Kuku sabzi is an herb-packed frittata that is traditionally eaten to welcome the arrival of spring in Iran. This version adds some cruciferous leafy greens to maximize the nutrient density. You can easily adapt this recipe to suit your tastes and experiment with using different herbs and greens. It is a fantastic way to use up any leftover, partial bunches of fresh herbs. (See page 178 for more info.)

🕐 **On the table in 15 minutes** | **Yield: 4–6 servings**

6 large eggs

½ tsp ground turmeric

½ tsp fine Himalayan salt

¼ tsp freshly cracked black pepper

2 large cloves garlic, minced

1 cup (60 g) finely chopped fresh parsley leaves

1 cup (16 g) finely chopped fresh cilantro

½ cup (26 g) finely chopped fresh dill

1 cup (20 g) finely chopped arugula or kale

1–2 green onions, thinly sliced

1 tbsp (15 ml) extra-virgin olive oil

Preheat the oven to 400°F (200°C).

In a large bowl, whisk the eggs with the turmeric, salt, pepper and garlic. Use a spoon to stir the parsley, cilantro, dill, arugula and green onions into the eggs to create a thick mixture just barely held together by the eggs.

Heat a 10- to 12-inch (25- to 30.5-cm) oven-safe skillet for several minutes over medium heat until hot. Pour in the olive oil and swirl to coat the bottom of the pan. Pour the egg mixture into the pan and use the spoon to spread it evenly. Cook until the edges are just set, about 3 to 4 minutes. Transfer the skillet to the heated oven and bake until it is set in the middle, about 7 minutes. Test it by shaking the pan and watch to see if the center wiggles. Broil on high for 1 or 2 minutes if necessary.

Cut it into 6 slices and serve immediately. Store leftovers in the refrigerator for up to 3 to 4 days. Reheat in a 350°F (180°C) oven for about 10 minutes or until warmed through, or serve leftovers chilled.

Sesame Ground Turkey Skillet

Ground turkey works so well in Asian-inspired dishes like this. It has a mild flavor so it soaks up all the flavors of the dish. This meal feels like something you'd order at a restaurant, but it is so easy to make at home! The basil and red bell pepper make this a beautiful dish and the sesame sauce packs a real punch of flavor that will leave you wanting seconds.

🕐 **On the table in 20 minutes** | **Yield: 4 servings**

FOR THE SAUCE

2½ tbsp (38 ml) lime juice

2 tbsp (30 ml) coconut aminos

2 tbsp (30 ml) toasted sesame oil

½ tsp ginger powder

1–2 tsp (3–6 g) toasted sesame seeds

1 tsp sriracha sauce (optional)

FOR THE TURKEY

1 tbsp (15 ml) avocado oil

1 lb (454 g) lean ground turkey

1 tsp fine Himalayan salt

1 red bell pepper, thinly sliced into bite-size strips

1 onion, cut into thin, half-moon strips

4 large cloves garlic, minced

1 cup (40 g) chiffonade-cut fresh basil

Butter lettuce (optional)

To make the sauce, in a small bowl, mix together the lime juice, coconut aminos, sesame oil, ginger, sesame seeds and sriracha sauce (if using). Set aside.

To cook the turkey, heat a large skillet for several minutes over medium heat until hot. Add the avocado oil and swirl to coat the pan. Crumble the ground turkey into the pan with the salt and cook until it's mostly browned, about 5 minutes. Add the bell pepper and onion and cook for about 10 minutes, or until the vegetables have softened. Add the garlic and cook about 1 minute, and then add the sauce and cook for 1 minute. Remove the pan from the heat and stir in the basil.

To serve as lettuce cups, remove the leaves from the butter lettuce and place 2 to 4 on each plate. Fill each with a few tablespoons of the turkey.

Chef's Notes: To make toasted sesame seeds, heat them in a dry pan over medium heat for about 3 to 5 minutes, stirring frequently to avoid burning. They will brown and become fragrant as they toast.

To perform a chiffonade cut for the basil leaves, stack them on top of each other and then roll them up from stem to leaf tip. Cut the roll crosswise into thin strips.

MAKE IT A MEAL: Pairs well with the Nutty Coleslaw on page 25.

Lemon-Garlic Chicken Skillet with Wilted Lettuce

This dish is the perfect fresh spring meal to me. The bright, bold flavor of the sauce is the perfect complement to the crisp and clean flavor of the lettuce. If you have never had wilted lettuce before, you are in for a treat! Many years ago, I was advised by my acupuncturist to avoid raw salad greens because according to Chinese medicine they are very hard on the digestive system. I am so happy I began cooking my lettuces back then because the flavor is amplified and the delicate texture is unique and delightful.

🕐 **On the table in 20 minutes** | **Yield: 3–4 servings**

FOR THE CHICKEN

1½ tbsp (23 ml) extra-virgin olive oil

2 large boneless, skinless chicken breasts, cut into 1" (2.5-cm) cubes (around 1¼ lbs [567 g])

¼ tsp fine Himalayan salt

FOR THE LEMON-GARLIC SAUCE

1 tsp finely grated lemon zest

¼ cup (60 ml) fresh lemon juice

2 tbsp (30 ml) Dijon mustard

4–5 large cloves garlic, minced

2 tsp (3 g) rubbed sage

½ tsp freshly cracked black pepper

½ tsp fine Himalayan salt

FOR SERVING

1 (12-oz [340-g]) head flavorful lettuce, like escarole or red leaf (can substitute baby spinach or arugula), rinsed and chopped

To make the chicken, heat a large skillet over medium heat for several minutes until hot. Add the oil and swirl the pan to coat the bottom. Add the chicken in a single layer to the hot skillet and sprinkle with the salt. Allow it to cook undisturbed for about 2 minutes, and then use a spatula to flip the pieces. Continue cooking, stirring occasionally, for another 3 to 5 minutes or until no pink remains on the outside.

To make the lemon-garlic sauce, while the chicken is cooking, add the lemon zest, lemon juice, mustard, garlic, sage, pepper and salt to a bowl. Whisk to form a thin sauce.

Add the lemon-garlic sauce to the pan and cook the chicken for 1 to 2 minutes. Test one or two of the larger pieces of chicken for doneness by using a spatula to cut it in half. There should be no pink remaining in the center and it should easily split into two.

Pour the cooked chicken and sauce out of the pan into a serving dish. Immediately add the lettuce to the pan and cook until wilted, about 2 minutes. You want there to still be some water on the leaves from rinsing to help them quickly wilt in the pan. Use a spatula to lift and flip the lettuce often so that it wilts down evenly. Divide the cooked lettuce among 3 or 4 plates and top each with the chicken and sauce.

MAKE IT A MEAL: Pairs well with Cauliflower Rice on page 80.

Chicken Caulifredo with Steamed Broccoli

What better way to use Caulifredo Sauce (page 165) than to make a veggie-packed chicken Alfredo? I know steamed broccoli can get a bad rap, but it all comes down to what you serve it with. In this case, broccoli gives body and depth of flavor to the dish and replaces the need for any type of noodle. It also perfectly soaks up and balances the richness of the Caulifredo Sauce and makes this meal a real nutrient powerhouse.

🕐 **On the table in 30 minutes** | **Yield: 4 servings**

4 small boneless, skinless chicken breasts (about 5–6 oz [142–170 g] each)

¾ tsp fine Himalayan salt

½ tsp freshly cracked black pepper

¼ tsp paprika, for color (optional)

1 tbsp (15 ml) avocado oil

2–3 crowns broccoli, florets only

About 3 cups (720 ml) Caulifredo Sauce (page 165)

Chopped parsley, to garnish

To make the chicken, pat the breasts dry and season them evenly on both sides with salt, pepper and paprika (if using). Heat a large skillet over medium heat for several minutes until hot. Add the oil and swirl the pan to coat the bottom. Cook the chicken without disturbing it for 5 to 7 minutes. It is ready to flip once it releases effortlessly from the pan and has a golden-brown crust. Cook it on the other side until the internal temperature reaches 165°F (74°C), about 5 to 7 minutes. Again, do not mess with the chicken while it is cooking. Allow it to rest for 3 minutes before slicing.

Once you add the chicken to the pan, prep the broccoli. To steam the broccoli, add about 1 inch (2.5 cm) of water to a saucepan with a steamer basket and bring it to a boil over high heat. If you don't own a steamer basket, you can just put the broccoli directly in the water. Once the water is boiling, add the broccoli and cover, steaming it for 5 minutes. Test to see if you can easily pierce the broccoli with a fork. If not, steam it for 1 or 2 minutes more, being careful not to overcook. If necessary, keep the broccoli warm while the rest of the dish finishes cooking by draining the water from the pan and holding the broccoli inside, with the lid slightly ajar.

To serve, divide the broccoli among 4 plates. Slice each chicken breast and arrange it on top of the broccoli, and then divide the Caulifredo Sauce among the plates and garnish with the parsley.

Time-Saving Tip: Prep the Caulifredo Sauce in advance to make this meal much faster and easier to pull together on a busy weeknight. If the sauce isn't prepared in advance, begin heating the pot for it at the same time you are heating the pan to cook the chicken.

Chef's Note: If using larger chicken breasts weighing 8 to 10 ounces (226 to 283 g), increase the cooking time up to 8 to 9 minutes per side.

Thai Turkey Burgers with Nutty Coleslaw

This dish is kind of like pad Thai in burger form, giving you the flavors you crave in a fast and weeknight-friendly format. The sauce mixed into the patties makes them tender, juicy and just bursting with flavor. And I think you're going to want to make this coleslaw to pair with other dishes, too!

🕐 **On the table in 30 minutes** | **Yield: 6 servings**

FOR THE COLESLAW

1 small head green or red cabbage, shredded (about 5–6 cups [350–420 g])

1 cup (110 g) peeled and shredded carrots (about 3 carrots)

3 tbsp (48 g) unsalted almond butter

2 tbsp (30 ml) coconut aminos

2 tbsp (30 ml) coconut or rice vinegar

½ tsp fine Himalayan salt

¼ tsp granulated garlic

¼ tsp ginger powder

FOR THE BURGERS

1½ tbsp (23 ml) avocado oil

¼ cup (64 g) unsalted almond butter

½ tsp fine Himalayan salt

¼ tsp granulated garlic

¼ tsp ginger powder

1 tbsp (15 ml) coconut aminos

1 tsp coconut vinegar

1 cup (110 g) peeled and shredded carrots (about 3 carrots)

2 green onions, thinly sliced

1 lb (454 g) ground turkey

FOR SERVING (OPTIONAL)

Sweet Potato Buns (page 66) or Portobello Buns (page 57)

To make the coleslaw, mix together the cabbage and carrots in a large bowl. In a second bowl, mix together the almond butter, coconut aminos, coconut vinegar, salt, garlic and ginger. Pour the sauce over the shredded vegetables. Use your hands to massage the vegetables for about 2 minutes. This makes the cabbage easier to digest and it also causes it to release some of its water into the sauce. Set it aside until the burgers are done.

To make the burgers, heat a large skillet over medium heat for several minutes until hot. Add the oil and swirl it to coat the bottom of the pan. In a large bowl, mix the almond butter, salt, garlic, ginger, coconut aminos and vinegar until a thick paste forms. Add the carrots and green onions and stir to combine. Mix in the ground turkey with your hands. Divide the mixture into 6 equal-sized portions and gently form them into patties about the size of your palm, about ½ inch (1 cm) thick.

Add the patties to the hot pan. They should sizzle when they hit the pan. Cook them for 4 to 6 minutes per side, until the outside is nice and brown and the internal temperature is 165°F (74°C). Serve with a generous portion of coleslaw and eat with a knife and fork, or serve them between Sweet Potato Buns or Portobello Buns.

Substitutions: To make these nut-free, use tahini instead of almond butter. Use rice vinegar for a more authentic flavor if you don't mind a rice-derived ingredient.

Huevos Ahogados with Plantain Tortillas

The name of this dish translates to "drowned eggs" and some call it "eggs drowned in salsa." You can also simply call it "salsa-poached eggs." No matter what you call it, it is an absolutely delicious breakfast and a great way to make humble eggs feel exotic and exciting. Skip the tortillas if you prefer a low-carb breakfast.

🕐 **On the table in 30 minutes** | **Yield: 6–8 servings**

2 green plantains

2 tbsp (30 ml) extra-virgin olive oil, plus extra for cooking

½ tsp fine Himalayan salt

1 batch of Shortcut Fire-Roasted Salsa (page 157)

6 eggs

Avocado, lime and chopped cilantro, for serving

Time-Saving Tip: Make the salsa a day in advance to allow the flavors to come together better, and to save time the morning you're making this dish. It can be on the table in as little as 15 minutes if you do this.

Chef's Note: Paleo tortillas are fairly widely available if you prefer not to make your own. You can also serve these with Paleo-friendly plantain chips.

Preheat the oven to 375°F (190°C).

To make the plantain tortillas, peel the plantains by slicing off the tips and cutting a slit down the length of the peel. Use your thumbs to lift away the peel. Chop each plantain into 4 pieces and add them to the bowl of a food processor with an S-blade attachment. Add the oil and salt. Process for about 1 minute, scraping the sides down at least once, to create a uniform batter. Lightly grease a metal baking sheet with olive oil. Scoop up about 2 tablespoons (30 g) of the plantain mixture and place it on the baking sheet. Dip a spoon in water or put a little olive oil on the back of it and use it to smooth the plantain mixture into a thin tortilla around 4 to 6 inches (10 to 15 cm) across. Repeat to make 6 to 8 tortillas, using 2 baking sheets if needed. Bake for 12 minutes or until the tops are no longer sticky.

To make the eggs, after putting the tortillas in the oven, pour the salsa into a 12-inch (30.5-cm) skillet and heat it over medium heat until it starts bubbling, about 8 minutes. Use a spatula to make a small well in the salsa, then crack an egg into it. Repeat with the remaining eggs. Simmer the eggs until they are done to your liking. You'll have firm whites and runny yolks after about 5 to 7 minutes. Once the whites set, you can occasionally spoon some of the salsa over the top to help the yolks cook. For jammy or firm yolks, continue cooking for up to about 12 minutes.

Serve immediately with avocado, lime and cilantro for a flavor-bomb breakfast.

Guacamole-Stuffed Chicken Poppers

It's incredible how the right five ingredients can come together to make an unforgettable dish. These tender chicken poppers have so much flavor infused from the classic trio of avocado, garlic and cilantro that you won't even want any kind of dipping sauce. Every time I make these, my husband and I fight over the last popper! They are a staple in our household, and you can easily double or triple the batch to have easy portable protein for the week ahead.

🕐 **On the table in 30 minutes** | **Yield: 3-4 servings**

1 packed cup (20 g) finely chopped cilantro (about 1 bunch)

1 ripe Hass avocado, peeled and pit removed

1 tbsp (9 g) minced garlic (about 3–4 large cloves)

1 tsp fine Himalayan salt

1 lb (454 g) ground chicken

2 tbsp (30 ml) avocado oil, divided

Lime slices, to serve

Add the cilantro and avocado to a mixing bowl and use a fork to mash the avocado into the cilantro. Add the garlic and salt and stir. Add the ground chicken to the mixture and stir to combine evenly.

Heat a 12-inch (30.5-cm) skillet for several minutes over medium heat until hot. Add 1 tablespoon (15 ml) of the oil and swirl the pan to coat it evenly. Cook the poppers in 2 batches. Use a tablespoon to pick up a scoop of the chicken mixture and drop it into the pan, gently flattening it with the back of the spoon. Add as many scoops as you can without overcrowding the poppers (around 7 to 10), and cook for 5 minutes. Flip the poppers and cook for 3 to 5 minutes, until the internal temperature reaches 165°F (74°C) and both sides have a nice golden-brown color.

Place the first batch on a paper towel–lined plate and cover to keep them warm while you cook the second batch. Add the remaining oil to the pan before cooking the second batch. Serve immediately with lime slices to squeeze over them. Leftovers can be reheated in a 350°F (180°C) oven for about 10 minutes.

Time-Saving Tip: To cut the cooking time in half, use 2 pans to cook all the poppers at once.

MAKE IT A MEAL: Pairs well with Roasted Carrot Fries with Carrot Top Chimichurri (page 116), because you can dip the popper in the sauce if you want.

Easy No-Breading Chicken Parmesan

This recipe was a special request from my husband, Andy, since it reminds him of growing up in Brooklyn. It's one of those iconic NYC dishes that is rooted in Italian cuisine, yet has become part of everyday life there. It's a fast and flavorful meal option in a hectic city. I chose to do an unbreaded chicken breast to make it simpler to prepare. I promise you won't feel like anything is missing when you make it (and Andy agrees!).

🕐 **On the table in 30 minutes** | **Yield: 4 servings**

4 small boneless, skinless chicken breasts (about 6 oz [170 g] each)

½ tsp fine Himalayan salt

¼ tsp freshly cracked black pepper

¼ tsp paprika

1 tbsp (15 ml) avocado oil

1 batch of 2-Minute Marinara (page 153)

1 batch of Herbed Fresh Mozzarella (page 162)

Preheat the oven to 425°F (220°C).

Pat the chicken dry and season both sides with the salt, pepper and paprika. Heat a large skillet over medium heat for several minutes until hot. Add the oil and swirl the pan to coat the bottom. Sear the chicken undisturbed for 3 to 4 minutes per side, or until the chicken releases effortlessly from the pan and has a golden crust on both sides. Transfer it to an 8 x 8–inch (20 x 20–cm) glass baking dish. Divide the marinara evenly on top of the breasts in the baking dish.

Divide the Herbed Fresh Mozzarella evenly on top of the 4 breasts. Bake for 12 to 15 minutes, or until the internal temperature of the thickest part of the chicken is 165°F (74°C). To brown the mozzarella, turn the broiler to high and cook for about 2 minutes.

Substitution: To make this nightshade-free, omit the paprika and use Beet Marinara (page 164) for the sauce.

MAKE IT A MEAL: Pairs well with Spaghetti Squash Noodles (page 73). Start cooking the squash first, before preparing the chicken.

BBQ Chicken Pizza with Plantain Crust

Green plantains are versatile starchy fruits that can replace flours in many recipes. (Check out my first cookbook, *Latin American Paleo Cooking*, for many more examples.) I love the simplicity of using them as a pizza crust. I think it's so much easier than measuring out a bunch of different flours, and I also notice that plantain crusts sit much better in my stomach than flour-based Paleo crusts. You can enjoy this dish with other topping options besides BBQ chicken. Don't forget about the 2-Minute Marinara (page 153) or even the Beet Marinara (page 164) that you could use instead with your favorite toppings.

On the table in 30 minutes | **Yield: 4 servings**

FOR THE CRUST

3 green plantains (about 1¾ lbs [794 g] before peeling)

½ tsp fine Himalayan salt

3 tbsp (45 ml) extra-virgin olive oil, plus extra for cooking

1 tsp granulated garlic

1 tsp granulated onion

1 tsp dried herbs of choice

FOR THE TOPPINGS

1 tsp avocado oil

1 large boneless, skinless chicken breast (about 8–9 oz [226–255 g])

Few pinches of fine Himalayan salt

¾–1 cup (180–240 ml) Memphis BBQ Sauce (page 161)

1 small red onion, thinly sliced into bite-size strips

1 batch of Fresh Mozzarella (either type, page 162)

Fresh cilantro, chopped, to garnish

Preheat the oven to 375°F (190°C).

To make the crust, peel the plantains by cutting off the tips and cutting a slit down the length of the peel. Use your thumbs to lift away the peel. Chop each plantain into 4 pieces and add them to the bowl of a food processor with the S-blade attachment. Add the salt and olive oil, granulated garlic, granulated onion and dried herbs of choice. Process for about 1 minute, scraping the sides down at least once, to create a uniform batter. Lightly grease a metal baking sheet with olive oil, and make sure your hands have some oil on them. Add the plantain batter and press it out to a thickness of between ¼ to ½ inch (0.6 to 1 cm). If it sticks to your hands, just put a little more oil on them. Bake the crust for 15 minutes, or until the top is set and no longer sticky.

To make the toppings, first cook the chicken. Heat a small skillet over medium heat for several minutes until hot. Add the avocado oil and swirl to coat the bottom of the pan. Pat the chicken breast dry and season both sides with salt. Sear it in the hot pan for 7 to 8 minutes per side, or until the internal temperature of the thickest part is 165°F (74°C). Do not move or disturb the chicken while it cooks. Let it rest for 3 minutes before slicing it into bite-size pieces.

(Continued)

BBQ Chicken Pizza with Plantain Crust (Continued)

To make the pizza, spread about half of the BBQ sauce over the top of the crust. In a small bowl, combine the chicken with the other half of the BBQ sauce and toss to coat it. Spread it evenly on top of the pizza and add the red onion. If you just made the Fresh Mozzarella, use a spoon to add dollops across the top of the pizza. If using refrigerated Fresh Mozzarella, break it off into small pieces to spread out across the pizza.

Bake for 10 to 15 minutes, or until everything is sizzling hot and the Fresh Mozzarella is melted. If you want to brown the Fresh Mozzarella, turn the broiler to high and cook for about 2 minutes, keeping a close eye to prevent it from burning. Sprinkle the cilantro generously on top of the pizza and serve immediately.

Time-Saving Tip: Make the magical, meltable Fresh Mozzarella (page 162) a day in advance to make putting together this pizza faster and easier.

Perfectly Crispy Chicken Thighs with Mushrooms and Honey Mustard

Who doesn't love the addictive crunch of perfectly crispy chicken skin? This is the optimal technique for cooking bone-in chicken thighs with the most tender, juicy meat topped with the crispiest skin. The secret is to start cooking the chicken on the stovetop in an oven-safe pan and then finish it off in the oven. While chicken and honey mustard is a classic flavor combo, you can use any sauce from the sauces chapter (page 151) that you like once you master the method. Cooking mushrooms in the same pan after the fat has rendered out of the skin allows them to soak up all that delicious flavor to make it a meal.

🕐 **On the table in less than 45 minutes** | **Yield: 2 servings**

FOR THE CHICKEN

4 bone-in, skin-on chicken thighs (about 1¼ lbs [567 g])

Few pinches of fine Himalayan salt and freshly cracked black pepper

Avocado oil

Preheat the oven to 400°F (200°C).

To make the chicken, thoroughly pat the thighs dry with paper towels. Season both sides with salt and pepper. Heat a large oven-safe skillet over medium heat for several minutes until hot. Add just enough avocado oil to coat the bottom of the pan. The skin is going to release a lot of fat, so you don't need much oil. Place the thighs skin-side down and don't touch them for 8 to 10 minutes, rotating the pan 180 degrees about halfway through to ensure even cooking. That uninterrupted contact with the hot pan is what renders out the fat and gives you the most delightfully crispy skin. Cover the skillet with a splatter screen if you have one.

The thighs are ready to flip when they easily release from the pan. Check at the 8 minute mark, but don't force them if they're not releasing on their own. Once they're ready, flip them over and sear the meaty side for about 1 minute, and then transfer the thighs to a plate with the skin side up.

(Continued)

Perfectly Crispy Chicken Thighs with Mushrooms and Honey Mustard (Continued)

FOR THE MUSHROOMS

1 shallot, chopped

8 oz (226 g) mushrooms (any variety), sliced

¼ tsp fine Himalayan salt

1 tsp crushed rosemary, or other favorite dried herb

FOR THE HONEY MUSTARD

1–1½ tbsp (15–23 ml) Dijon or yellow mustard

1 tbsp (15 ml) mayonnaise

1 tbsp (15 ml) honey

To make the mushrooms, add the shallot to the pan and cook for 30 seconds. Add the mushrooms, salt and rosemary and cook, stirring often, for about 2 minutes, until the mushrooms have shrunk and a good bit of their water has cooked off. Push the mushrooms to the edge of the skillet and then place the thighs skin-side up in the center of the pan. Roast them in the oven for 15 to 20 minutes, or until the internal temperature at the thickest part is 165°F (74°C). If you want to make the skin extra crispy, remove the mushrooms from the pan and broil the chicken on high for about 2 minutes.

To make the honey mustard sauce, in a small bowl, mix together the mustard, mayonnaise and honey. Taste the sauce with just 1 tablespoon (15 ml) of mustard before adding the extra ½ tablespoon (8 ml). Technically, you can enjoy a yummy sauce with just equal parts honey and mustard, but adding the mayo makes it more like a traditional dressing.

MAKE IT A MEAL: Pairs well with Spiced Beet Greens (page 104), Sautéed Zucchini Coins with Basil (page 93) or Ethiopian Cabbage (page 100).

Ranch Chicken Drumsticks with Cabbage Steaks

Drumsticks do well when cooked similarly to chicken wings: nice and hot to help the skin get crispy. This quick and easy ranch seasoning blend gives them great flavor, and you can use this blend to season other things as well. The cabbage steaks are a perfect side for this dish since they cook for the same amount of time, but I hope you experiment and make them with other proteins, too.

🕐 **On the table in a little over 45 minutes** | **Yield: 2–3 servings**

FOR THE CHICKEN

6 chicken drumsticks (about 1¼ lbs [567 g])

½ tsp granulated garlic

½ tsp granulated onion

½ tsp dried dill weed

½ tsp fine Himalayan salt

¼ tsp freshly cracked black pepper

FOR THE CABBAGE STEAKS

1 small green cabbage

2–3 tbsp (30–45 ml) extra-virgin olive oil

Few pinches of fine Himalayan salt and freshly cracked black pepper

Preheat the oven to 425°F (220°C).

To make the chicken, pat it dry with paper towels. In a large bowl, mix together the garlic, onion, dill weed, salt and pepper. Toss the drumsticks with the seasonings to evenly coat the chicken, and then arrange them on a metal baking sheet.

To make the cabbage steaks, cut the cabbage vertically into 1-inch (2.5-cm)-thick slices. You should get about 6 total. Place them on a baking sheet and drizzle with the olive oil. Use your hands to rub it into both sides of the steaks. Use additional oil if necessary to coat each steak well. Sprinkle with salt and pepper.

Place the chicken in the oven on the middle rack and the cabbage on the lower rack and bake for 20 minutes. Remove both and carefully flip everything to the other side, and then switch the position of the pans in the oven and bake for another 15 to 20 minutes, until the chicken skin is crispy and the internal temperature at the thickest part is 165°F (74°C). The cabbage steaks should be nice and caramelized on top and fork tender.

Baked BBQ Chicken Thighs Three Ways

Growing up in Georgia, and now living in Memphis, Tennessee, means that good BBQ is true comfort food to me. There are so many regional differences in BBQ sauce, and I am here for all of them. I've chosen my three favorite kinds of sauce to include in this book that I believe will radically enhance your Paleo dining experiences. The best part is that each sauce comes together in mere minutes, but you don't have to tell anyone that secret.

On the table in less than 45 minutes | **Yield: 4 servings**

Avocado oil, for cooking

8 boneless, skinless chicken thighs (about 2–2½ lbs [0.9–1 kg])

1½ tsp (9 g) fine Himalayan salt

1–1½ cups (240–360 ml) BBQ sauce of choice, divided

Preheat the oven to 425°F (220°C).

Lightly grease a large metal baking sheet with the oil, and then pat the chicken dry and place it on the sheet. Season both sides of each thigh with the salt. Set aside half of the sauce to serve with the cooked chicken. Divide the remaining sauce in half again, and use 1 portion to generously brush both sides of each thigh. Bake for 15 minutes. Brush the tops with the second portion of sauce, and bake for 15 minutes more, or until the chicken is cooked through. Serve immediately with extra BBQ sauce on the side.

Chef's Note: You can choose any or all of the BBQ sauces in this book: Memphis BBQ Sauce (page 161), Carolina Mustard BBQ Sauce (page 155) and/or White BBQ Sauce (page 158).

Substitution: If you prefer to make baked BBQ chicken breasts, substitute about 4 large boneless, skinless breasts and cook for only 22 to 25 minutes, brushing them with extra sauce halfway through cooking. Check the internal temperature is 165°F (74°C) with a thermometer to avoid overcooking.

MAKE IT A MEAL: Pairs well with Crispy Baked Rosemary Garlic Steak Fries (page 120) or Herbed Beet and Turnip Wedges (page 123).

Sheet Pan Chicken and Crispy Broccoli

When I asked my husband, Andy, for the top three recipes he wanted to see in this cookbook, his number one choice was Chinese-style chicken and broccoli. I wanted to make a sheet pan version with a flavorful sauce and tender, juicy chicken that doesn't require marinating or using starch. I am so happy with this recipe, and it's already been on repeat for us since I wrote it!

🕐 **On the table in less than 45 minutes** | **Yield: 4 servings**

FOR THE CHICKEN

8 boneless, skinless chicken thighs (about 2–2½ lbs [0.9–1 kg])

2 tsp (10 ml) avocado oil, to coat thighs

1 tsp granulated garlic

1½ tsp (9 g) fine Himalayan salt

1 tsp freshly cracked black pepper

FOR THE CRISPY BROCCOLI

2–3 large crowns broccoli, florets only

2 tbsp (30 ml) avocado oil

½ tsp granulated garlic

Few pinches of fine Himalayan salt

FOR THE SAUCE

¼ cup (60 ml) coconut aminos

2 tbsp (30 ml) coconut vinegar

1 tsp toasted sesame oil

½ cup (120 ml) water

2 tsp (0.25 oz) gelatin

4 large cloves garlic, minced

2 tbsp (28 g) minced fresh ginger

2 green onions, thinly sliced, to garnish

Preheat the oven to 425°F (220°C) and make sure one rack is in the center of the oven and the other is near the bottom.

To make the chicken, pat the chicken thighs dry and place them on a metal sheet pan. Drizzle the avocado oil over the chicken. Use your hands to rub the oil over both sides of each thigh. Season both sides with the granulated garlic, salt and pepper.

To make the broccoli, place the broccoli florets on another baking sheet, drizzle them with avocado oil and sprinkle with the granulated garlic and salt. Use your hands to massage everything together to ensure the florets are coated with oil. For tender broccoli, don't add it to the oven until after the chicken has cooked for 15 minutes, and place it on the bottom rack.

For very crispy broccoli, place the pan with the chicken on the middle rack and the broccoli on the bottom rack. Bake for 15 minutes, and then swap the positions of the pans and bake for 15 minutes more. Allow the chicken to rest on the pan outside the oven for 3 minutes before slicing.

To make the sauce, about 5 minutes before the chicken and broccoli are done cooking, add the coconut aminos, vinegar, sesame oil, water, gelatin, garlic and ginger to a small saucepan. When adding the gelatin, slowly sprinkle it so that it can bloom (absorb liquid). This helps prevent it from forming clumps. Heat the saucepan over medium heat until it starts steaming, whisking to dissolve the gelatin, and then remove it from the heat.

Add the broccoli to a large serving bowl. Slice the chicken and add it along with the sauce and toss everything to combine. Divide into 4 servings and garnish with sliced green onions.

Crispy Brazilian Chicken Wings with Avocado Crema

This recipe is an adaptation of one of the most popular recipes on my website. This version simplifies the seasonings and doesn't require any flour, making it faster to prepare on a busy evening as well as low-carb. This mix of spices (not including the baking soda and cream of tartar) is known as *tempero baiano* and is one I keep mixed up in a spice jar for easy access. The secret to super crispy skin without deep frying the wings is the mix of baking soda and cream of tartar. You can make the wings without adding it, but they won't be as crispy.

🕐 **On the table in a little over 45 minutes** | **Yield: 2 servings**

1 tsp ground cumin

1 tsp dried oregano

¾ tsp white pepper

¾ tsp turmeric powder

1 tsp fine Himalayan salt

1 tsp cream of tartar

½ tsp baking soda

½ tsp granulated garlic

¼ tsp ground coriander seeds

⅛ tsp cayenne pepper

1½ lbs (680 g) chicken wings, separated into flats and drumettes

Avocado oil, for cooking

1 batch of Avocado Crema (page 156)

Lime wedges, for serving (optional)

Preheat the oven to 425°F (220°C).

In a large bowl, mix together the cumin, oregano, pepper, turmeric, salt, cream of tartar, baking soda, garlic, coriander and cayenne. Pat the wings dry with paper towels, then toss them with the seasonings in the bowl until they are evenly coated.

Use the avocado oil to lightly grease a metal baking sheet with a rim and place the wings on it with the thickest skin side facing down. Roast them for 20 minutes, and then flip all the pieces over, using a spatula if necessary to release them. Roast them for 15 to 20 minutes more, until they are nice and crispy and cooked through.

Serve the wings with crema on the side for dipping, or drizzle it on top of them before serving. Serve with lime wedges, if desired.

Substitution: If white pepper is unavailable, use ½ teaspoon of black pepper and ¼ teaspoon of dry mustard powder.

MAKE IT A MEAL: Pairs well with Garlicky Mustard Greens (page 96) or Fried Ripe Plantains (page 62).

BEEF, PORK AND LAMB

For weeknight-friendly meals made from beef, pork or lamb, you're limited on the number of cuts of meat that you can utilize, since things like roasts, ribs, legs, oxtail and the like require long cooking times for tender meat. But that doesn't mean that fast weeknight meals have to be boring or feel repetitive. In this chapter, you will find a huge range of globally inspired dishes that will keep meals exciting from week to week using a variety of quick-cooking cuts.

← See recipe on page 61.

Cajun-Blackened Pork Chops

New Orleans will always be a second home to me. I attended Tulane University for both undergrad and grad school for neuroscience, and while there, I fell in love with the city's cuisine. This Cajun blackening seasoning mimics one of my favorite store-bought blends from the city and is so good on everything, especially chicken and white fish. It's even a great way to jazz up green veggies and fries. You name it, I pretty much guarantee this seasoning will be good on it!

On the table in less than 15 minutes | **Yield: 4 servings**

FOR THE CAJUN BLACKENING SEASONING

½ tsp fine Himalayan salt

½ tsp freshly cracked black pepper

¼ tsp garlic powder

¼ tsp cayenne pepper

¼ tsp paprika

¼ tsp dried oregano

¼ tsp dried thyme

FOR THE PORK CHOPS

1 tbsp (15 ml) avocado oil

4 boneless pork loin chops, about 1" (2.5 cm) thick (about 5–6 oz [142–170 g] each)

To make the seasoning, mix together the salt, pepper, garlic, cayenne, paprika, oregano and thyme in a bowl.

To make the pork chops, heat a large skillet for several minutes over medium heat until hot. Add the oil and swirl to coat the bottom of the pan. Season both sides of each chop generously with the seasoning. Sear the chops in the pan for 4 to 5 minutes per side, or until they reach the desired level of doneness (at least 145°F [63°C]). Let the chops rest for 3 minutes before cutting and serving.

Chef's Note: Quadruple the seasoning mixture and store it in an empty spice jar to have on hand any time you want to use it. Trust me, you're going to want to put it on everything!

MAKE IT A MEAL: Pairs well with Ethiopian Cabbage (page 100), as pictured, Fried Ripe Plantains (page 62) or Lemon-Garlic Brussels Sprout Chips (page 99).

Maple-Sage Pork Breakfast Sausage

There is nothing like the rich, buttery flavor of maple syrup paired with savory pork for breakfast. This has been my favorite breakfast sausage recipe for years! It also freezes really well if you want to keep a stash on hand for easy breakfasts. You can reheat the patties by placing them in a cold oven and then heating it to 350°F (180°C); by the time the oven reaches temp they're usually warmed up and ready for you. So easy!

On the table in 15 minutes | **Yield: 4 servings**

1 tbsp (15 ml) avocado oil or lard

1 tsp fine Himalayan salt

1 tsp rubbed sage

½ tsp dried thyme

½ tsp freshly cracked black pepper

¼ tsp cayenne

⅛ tsp ground coriander

1 lb (454 g) ground pork

1½–2 tbsp (23–30 ml) dark robust maple syrup

Heat a large skillet over medium heat until hot. Add the oil and swirl the pan to coat the bottom.

While the pan is heating, mix together the salt, sage, thyme, pepper, cayenne and coriander in a small bowl. Place the ground pork in a medium bowl with the maple syrup and sprinkle the seasoning on top, gently working it in with your hands.

To make patties, form the ground meat into 6 to 8 evenly sized patties and cook them in the heated pan for about 4 to 5 minutes per side, until they're browned on both sides and the internal temperature is 160°F (70°C).

To make ground sausage, add the meat mixture to the heated pan and use a spatula to break it into crumbles as it cooks. Cook until well browned and cooked through, about 8 to 10 minutes. If you want to make it a meal, just follow the instructions for Sausage Sawmill Gravy with Fried Ripe Plantains (page 62).

> **Chef's Note:** You can use ½ teaspoon of crushed red pepper flakes as a substitute for the cayenne pepper if preferred.

Pork Tenderloin Medallions with Horseradish Pan Sauce

Pork tenderloin can make a delicious roast, but I prefer to slice it into medallions and quickly sear them on the stovetop with a flavorful pan sauce. Horseradish is an underutilized seasoning in my opinion. Not only does it wake your taste buds up with its heat, but it is also a cruciferous vegetable and compared to broccoli, it has up to 10-times the concentration of the cancer-fighting compounds known as glucosinolates. It's also a fantastic way to add heat to dishes without nightshades, which some people can be sensitive to, especially in the case of autoimmunity. If you don't already cook with horseradish, I think you'll really enjoy adding it into the mix with the recipes in this book.

🕐 **On the table in 15 minutes** | **Yield: 4 servings**

FOR THE MEDALLIONS

1–1¼ lbs (454–567 g) pork tenderloin, cut into ½" (1-cm) medallions (about 12–16 medallions)

Few pinches of fine Himalayan salt

Few pinches of freshly cracked black pepper

1½ tbsp (21 g) lard or ghee

FOR THE PAN SAUCE

1 shallot, finely diced

½ cup (120 ml) water or bone broth

1 tbsp (15 ml) Dijon mustard

2 tbsp (30 g) prepared horseradish

½ tsp dried rosemary

½ tsp fine Himalayan salt

To make the medallions, flatten each pork slice between the palms of your hands with firm pressure to make them all an even thickness. Pat them dry with a paper towel so that a nice crust forms when you sear them. Season them on both sides with a few pinches of salt and pepper.

Heat a large skillet for several minutes over medium heat until hot. Melt the lard and swirl the pan to coat the bottom. Sear the medallions for 2 to 3 minutes per side, and then transfer them to a plate while you cook the sauce.

To make the sauce, add the shallot to the skillet and cook for about 2 minutes. Pour in the water or broth to deglaze the skillet, using a spatula to scrape up any browned bits. Add the mustard, horseradish, rosemary and salt and bring the sauce to a bubble. Lower the heat and simmer it for a few minutes to allow the sauce to reduce and slightly thicken. Add the medallions back to the pan and toss in the sauce, then serve.

Chef's Note: Read the labels of prepared horseradish to ensure you get one that's only horseradish and vinegar. Some brands add non-Paleo additives like soybean oil.

MAKE IT A MEAL: Pairs well with Warm Lemon-Dill Cucumbers (page 89), Sautéed Zucchini Coins with Basil (page 93) or Smoky Roasted Asparagus (page 97).

Spicy Italian Sausage

Sausage for dinner is about as easy as it gets for your main protein. You can serve it ground or in patties, or you can use it to make the Zuppa Toscana on page 133. I almost never buy pre-made sausages anymore, since it is so easy to make your own and you can make them exactly the way you want them. It saves money, too!

🕐 **On the table in 15 minutes** | **Yield: 4 servings**

2 tsp (30 ml) avocado oil or lard

1 tsp fine Himalayan salt

1 tsp freshly cracked black pepper

1 tsp dried basil

1 tsp granulated garlic

1 tsp paprika

½ tsp cayenne pepper

½ tsp fennel seeds

⅛ tsp dried oregano

⅛ tsp dried thyme

1 lb (454 g) ground pork

Heat a large skillet over medium heat until hot. Add the oil and swirl the pan to coat the bottom.

While the pan is heating, mix together the salt, pepper, basil, garlic, paprika, cayenne, fennel, oregano and thyme in a small bowl. Place the ground pork in a medium bowl and sprinkle the seasoning on top, gently working it in with your hands.

To make patties, form the ground meat into 4 to 8 evenly sized patties and cook them in the heated pan for about 4 to 5 minutes per side, until they're browned on both sides and the internal temperature is 160°F (70°C).

To make ground sausage, add the pork to the heated pan and use a spatula to break it into crumbles as it cooks. Cook until well browned and cooked through, about 8 to 10 minutes.

Chef's Note: If you do not like the licorice flavor of fennel seeds, simply omit them. The sausage is still incredibly delicious without fennel.

Time-Saving Tip: Scale up the spice blend recipe and store it in an empty spice jar to make future meals even faster and easier. You'll use about 2 tablespoons (5 g) of the mix for every 1 pound (454 g) of ground pork.

MAKE IT A MEAL: Use as the base for Zuppa Toscana (page 133).

Ground Beef Stroganoff with Cauliflower Rice

Is it weird that I used to look forward to beef stroganoff day at school when I was a kid? I didn't care much for the beef in it, just the noodles slathered in the rich and creamy sauce. This sauce is better than I remember, which is a feat without any flour or dairy. And noodles? Who needs them! I'd much rather have this served over a big pile of cauliflower rice. Using ground beef in this dish makes it weeknight friendly and easy on the food budget, too.

🕐 **On the table in less than 30 minutes** | **Yield: 4 servings**

2 tsp (10 ml) melted ghee or avocado oil

1 lb (454 g) ground beef

1 batch of Cauliflower Rice (page 80)

1 tsp fine Himalayan salt

8 oz (226 g) cremini or baby bella mushrooms, sliced

1 small white onion, chopped

4 large cloves garlic, minced

1–1½ cups (240–360 ml) beef broth

½ tsp freshly cracked black pepper

1 tbsp (15 ml) coconut aminos

1 tbsp (15 ml) Dijon mustard

1 tbsp (15 ml) lemon juice

¼–½ cup (60–120 ml) canned full-fat coconut milk

Chopped parsley, to garnish

Preheat the oven to 400°F (200°C).

Heat a large sauté pan with straight sides for several minutes over medium heat until hot. Add the ghee or oil and swirl to coat the bottom of the pan. Add the ground beef and break it into large pieces. Let it brown undisturbed for about 5 minutes.

While the beef cooks, start the Cauliflower Rice (page 80).

Break the beef into smaller crumbles and sprinkle with the salt, stirring every minute or so and cooking for about 3 to 5 minutes more, until no signs of pink remain. Add the mushrooms, onion and garlic and cook for 4 minutes. Add the broth, pepper, coconut aminos, mustard and lemon juice. Simmer for about 5 minutes to reduce the sauce. Stir in the coconut milk at the very end, to taste and to desired level of creaminess. Divide the cauliflower rice among 4 bowls and serve with a generous amount of stroganoff on top. Garnish with the parsley.

Chef's Note: This dish is also great served over cooked spaghetti squash strands. See page 73 for cooking instructions. You'll need to start cooking the spaghetti squash before the beef.

Mediterranean-Herbed Lamb Burgers with Tzatziki Sauce

Burgers are the perfect fast and budget-friendly weeknight meal, and this is my go-to recipe for ground lamb because it is THAT good. The patties are packed with unique flavor from the trio of fresh herbs and lemon zest, and the tzatziki sauce is rich and creamy and the perfect condiment to slather on top. You can enjoy these burgers with a knife and fork or serve with one of my bun options if you're feeling fancy.

🕐 **On the table in less than 30 minutes** | **Yield: 4 burgers**

FOR THE TZATZIKI SAUCE

2 small Persian cucumbers (about 5 oz [142 g])

4 large cloves garlic, peeled

2 tbsp (7 g) chopped fresh dill fronds

10 big mint leaves

2 tbsp (30 ml) fresh lemon juice (about 1 lemon)

¼ cup (60 ml) canned full-fat coconut milk

¼ cup (60 ml) mayonnaise

½ tsp raw apple cider vinegar

½ tsp fine Himalayan salt

¼ tsp freshly cracked black pepper

Make the sauce first so that it can chill and thicken in the fridge while you cook the burgers. Make sure to zest the lemon for the burgers before squeezing the juice for the sauce.

To quickly make a thin tzatziki sauce, place the cucumbers, garlic, dill fronds, mint leaves, lemon juice, coconut milk, mayonnaise, apple cider vinegar, salt and pepper in a food processor with the S-blade attachment. Pulse until everything is puréed. For a thicker, more traditionally textured sauce, finely dice the cucumbers, garlic, dill and mint. Set aside. Add the lemon juice, coconut milk, mayonnaise, apple cider vinegar, salt and pepper to a bowl and whisk together with a fork. Stir in the diced cucumbers and herbs. Place in the refrigerator.

(Continued)

Mediterranean-Herbed Lamb Burgers with Tzatziki Sauce (Continued)

FOR THE BURGERS

1 lb (454 g) ground lamb

2 tbsp (2 g) chopped fresh cilantro or dill fronds

2 tbsp (11 g) chopped fresh mint (about 12 big leaves)

2 tbsp (8 g) chopped fresh flat-leaf parsley

4 cloves garlic, minced

½ tsp finely grated lemon zest

½ tsp fine Himalayan salt

¼ tsp freshly cracked black pepper

2 tsp (10 ml) avocado oil

FOR SERVING

1 lb (454 g) rinsed, chopped leafy greens, such as kale, chard, collards, etc. (optional)

Fine Himalayan salt and freshly cracked black pepper, to taste

Sweet Potato Buns (page 66) or Portobello Buns (page 57) (optional)

To make the burgers, add the lamb, cilantro, mint, parsley, garlic, lemon zest, salt and pepper to a bowl. Combine with your hands. Form the mixture into 4 patties about the size of your palm. Heat a large skillet for several minutes over medium heat until hot. Add the oil and swirl to coat the bottom of the pan. Cook the burgers for about 5 minutes per side, or until browned on both sides and the internal temperature is 160°F (70°C).

After the burgers have cooked, add the chopped greens to the pan (if using) to cook down in the flavorful fat left in the pan. It should only take a few minutes, the perfect amount of time to allow the burgers to rest before eating. Season with salt and pepper and serve with the burgers. Serve the burgers on sweet potato or portobello buns (if using).

Chef's Note: Store leftover fresh herbs in a jar with water (like a bouquet of flowers) in the fridge and cover with a plastic or mesh bag to prevent wilting. Use the leftover herbs to make the Persian Herb Frittata (Kuku Sabzi) (page 17) so nothing goes to waste.

Better-Than-Fast-Food Burgers

These burgers have all the features of a classic fast food burger but they're made with healthy ingredients. Rich and creamy special sauce—that is surprisingly easy to make—paired with thin, crisp patties will bring back memories for sure! The savory portobello buns really tie it all together, but bring plenty of napkins to the table, or just plan on eating with a knife and fork.

🕐 **On the table in 30 minutes** | **Yield: 4 servings**

FOR THE PORTOBELLO BUNS

Avocado oil, for cooking

8 large portobello mushroom caps, wiped clean with a damp cloth

FOR THE BURGERS

1 lb (454 g) ground beef

Few pinches of fine Himalayan salt and freshly cracked black pepper

1 tbsp (15 ml) avocado oil

Preheat the oven to 425°F (220°C).

To make the portobello buns, lightly grease a large baking sheet with the avocado oil and place the portobello caps gill-side up. Bake for 10 minutes, and then flip and bake for 10 minutes. Carefully pat dry with paper towels if there is any liquid on them.

To make the burgers, while the mushrooms are cooking, divide the beef into eight 2-ounce (57-g) portions. Roll them into balls and flatten them as thin as possible, so that they're about ¼ inch (6 mm) thick and about the size of your palm. You can do this between 2 pieces of parchment paper to help the patties hold their shape. Season both sides with salt and pepper.

Heat a large skillet over medium heat for several minutes until hot. It is critical for the pan to be properly heated for the burgers to get the right texture. Add the avocado oil and swirl it around the pan to coat the bottom. Cook the patties for about 2 to 3 minutes. Flip and cook the other sides for less than a minute.

(Continued)

Better-Than-Fast-Food Burgers (Continued)

FOR THE SPECIAL SAUCE

1 tbsp (15 ml) mayonnaise

1 tbsp (15 ml) ketchup

1 tbsp (15 ml) mustard (yellow, Dijon or stone ground)

½ tbsp (8 ml) coconut aminos

1–2 tsp (2–5 g) minced dill pickle (optional)

OPTIONAL TOPPINGS

Sliced tomatoes

Shredded lettuce

Sliced red onion

Dill pickle slices

Cooked bacon slices

To make the sauce, in a small bowl, mix together the mayonnaise, ketchup, mustard, coconut aminos and pickle (if using).

To assemble the burgers, place 2 patties between 2 portobello buns with all the toppings you want. Be sure to add a generous dollop of the special sauce in between the patties.

Time-Saving Tip: You can also use lettuce to wrap up the burgers to significantly reduce the total prep time of this dish. Two leaves of romaine lettuce laid at a right angle work well. Fold one stem-end up, then the other, and finally the tops of each leaf.

MAKE IT A MEAL: If you don't mind waiting for them to cook, definitely make a batch of Crispy Baked Rosemary Garlic Steak Fries (page 120) to pair with these burgers. Start cooking them first, and then cook the portobello buns when the fries are about halfway done. Then quickly cook up the patties.

Mongolian Beef with Steamed Broccoli

Mongolian beef used to be my go-to Chinese takeout dish. Restaurants usually serve it with a starchy, sugar-sweetened sauce, but it's easy to make a healthier, unsweetened version with Paleo ingredients. Coconut aminos have a hint of natural sweetness that intensifies as they cook down, negating the need to add a sweetener.

🕐 **On the table in less than 30 minutes** | **Yield: 4–5 servings**

2 crowns broccoli, florets only

2 tbsp (30 ml) avocado oil, divided

1–1¼ lbs (454–567 g) flank steak, sliced very thin against the grain, strips cut in half or thirds crosswise

Few pinches of fine Himalayan salt

6 green onions, cut in 2" (5-cm) pieces, whites and greens separated

4 cloves garlic, minced

1 tbsp (6 g) minced ginger

½–1 tsp crushed red pepper flakes (optional)

¼ cup (60 ml) coconut aminos

2 tbsp (30 ml) water

1–2 tsp (3–5 g) tapioca starch, to thicken sauce (optional)

You can cook the broccoli and beef simultaneously. Make sure you have all of your ingredients prepped because this recipe moves quickly once you start cooking it.

To make the broccoli, add about 1 inch (2.5 cm) of water to a saucepan with a steamer basket and bring to a boil over high heat. If you don't own a steamer basket, you can just put the broccoli directly in the water. Once boiling, add the broccoli and cover, steaming for 5 minutes. Test to see if you can easily pierce the broccoli with a fork. If not, steam for 1 or 2 minutes longer, being careful not to overcook. If necessary, keep the broccoli warm while the beef finishes cooking by draining the water from the pan and holding the broccoli inside, with the lid slightly ajar.

To make the beef, heat a large skillet over medium-high heat until very hot. Add 1 tablespoon (15 ml) of the avocado oil and swirl it around the bottom of the pan. Working in batches so you don't crowd the slices in the pan, quickly sear the steak slices for about 1 to 2 minutes per side, seasoning each batch with a pinch or two of salt. Set the steak aside in a bowl with all the pan drippings.

Add the remaining avocado oil to the pan and cook the onion whites for about 2 minutes. Add the garlic, ginger and red pepper flakes (if using) and cook until fragrant, less than 1 minute. Pour in the coconut aminos and water and scrape the bottom of the pan to release any browned bits. If using tapioca starch, sprinkle it into the sauce. Let the sauce simmer for 1 to 2 minutes. Add the steak to the pan along with the green onion slices and cook for about 2 minutes. Serve immediately with a generous portion of broccoli on the side.

Sausage Sawmill Gravy with Fried Ripe Plantains

This combo of classic dishes is what happens when a Georgia Peach marries a Puerto Rican—a unique and absolutely delicious kind of fusion cuisine! Sawmill gravy is a beloved Southern breakfast item and combines the flavor of breakfast sausage with the creamy goodness of gravy. It is easy to make in one pan, and while it is traditionally served on top of open-faced biscuits, I can't get enough of it served on top of fried ripe plantains. Trust me, it's incredible!

On the table in 30 minutes | **Yield: 4 servings**

FOR THE FRIED RIPE PLANTAINS

2–3 ripe plantains (yellow and black peels, flesh should give when you press but not be mushy)

2 tbsp (30 g) lard, bacon grease or avocado oil

FOR THE SAWMILL GRAVY

1 lb (454 g) uncooked Maple-Sage Pork Breakfast Sausage (page 48) or your favorite store-bought sausage

½ tbsp (8 g) lard, bacon grease or avocado oil

1 (13.5-oz [400-g]) can full-fat coconut milk

1 tbsp (8 g) tapioca starch plus 2 tbsp (30 ml) water, fully dissolved into a slurry

½ tsp fine Himalayan salt

½ tsp freshly cracked black pepper

To prepare the plantains, peel each one by slicing both tips off with a knife, and then cut a slit in the skin down the length of the plantain. Lift away the peel with your fingers. Slice the plantains into pieces about ¾ inch (2 cm) thick. You can either slice them into discs or cut along the bias (diagonal) for oblong-shaped pieces. Set aside.

If making the breakfast sausage from scratch, mix together all of the ingredients on page 48.

The plantains and gravy take about the same amount of time to cook, so you can use 2 pans to cook them simultaneously. Heat 2 large skillets for several minutes over medium heat until hot. Add the lard to each and swirl to coat the bottoms of the pans.

In one pan, crumble the sausage with a spatula and cook until it is well-browned, about 8 to 10 minutes. Use a slotted spoon to transfer the cooked sausage crumbles to a bowl, leaving the fat behind in the pan. Pour in the coconut milk and scrape up any browned bits from the bottom of the pan with the spatula. Pour the tapioca slurry into the pan with the salt and pepper and cook for several minutes until the gravy thickens. Add the cooked sausage back in and cook a minute more to allow the flavors to meld.

In the second pan, carefully add the plantain slices to the heated fat (they will sizzle) and cook them on each side for about 3 to 5 minutes, or until they have turned a nice golden brown color and have partially caramelized. Be careful not to burn them. Transfer to a paper towel–lined plate to drain. Divide the plantains among 4 plates and serve them smothered with the gravy.

Mozzarella Meatza

I will admit that the first time I heard about a "meatza," I didn't think it sounded appetizing. But then I tried one, and I understood why they are so popular! I actually really love ground beef as a topping on pizza, so of course it tastes delicious to use ground beef as the crust to load up with your favorite veggie toppings. My magical, meltable Fresh Mozzarella (page 162) is the crown jewel on top of this incredible meal.

🕐 **On the table in 30 minutes** | **Yield: 4 servings**

1 lb (454 g) 10- or 15-percent-fat ground beef

1 tsp fine Himalayan salt

1 tsp dried basil

1 tsp dried oregano

½ tsp freshly cracked black pepper

1 batch of Fresh Mozzarella (page 162), either version

1 batch of 2-Minute Marinara (page 153) or your favorite pizza sauce

¼ cup (45 g) sliced Kalamata olives

1 small red bell pepper, thinly sliced

1 small red onion, thinly sliced

Preheat the oven to 400°F (200°C).

To make the crust, in a bowl, mix together the beef, salt, basil, oregano and pepper. Line a metal baking sheet with parchment paper and place the meat in the middle. Spread the meat into an even circle about ¼ inch (6 mm) thick. You can place a second piece of parchment paper on top and use a rolling pin if needed. Bake the crust for 10 minutes. Drain the rendered fat into the trash. Pat the top of the crust dry with paper towels.

While the crust is cooking, make the Fresh Mozzarella (page 162) and 2-Minute Marinara (page 153).

Spread the marinara sauce over the top of the crust and add the olives, bell pepper and onion. If using freshly cooked Herbed Fresh Mozzarella, use a spoon to drop dollops of it all around the crust. If using chilled, break it off into small pieces and place them over the top. Bake for 12 to 15 minutes. If you want, you can broil for 1 to 2 minutes to really melt and brown the cheese.

Substitutions: Use the Beet Marinara (page 164) and use another veggie in place of the sliced peppers to make the meatza nightshade-free. Time to table will be longer if you are making it from scratch. Leftover Roasted Mushrooms with Gremolata (page 108) are perfect to use as a topping.

Memphis BBQ Sloppy Joes with Sweet Potato Buns

One of the only ways I would ever eat beef as a child was inside a sloppy Joe sandwich. I was all about that tangy, sweet sauce! Some people like to use a BBQ sauce on their sloppy Joes, and that is what I decided to do for this recipe. My Memphis BBQ Sauce is absolutely perfect in this dish, having just the right amount of natural sweetness from the dates and zing from the spices to make it better than what you remember eating as a kid.

🕐 **On the table in less than 30 minutes** | **Yield: 4 servings**

FOR THE SWEET POTATO BUNS

1 large sweet potato (the thicker, the better)

2 tsp (10 ml) coconut oil or avocado oil

FOR THE SLOPPY JOE FILLING

2 tsp (10 ml) avocado oil

1 lb (454 g) ground beef

½ tsp fine Himalayan salt

1 small white onion, chopped

1 red bell pepper, chopped

1½ cups (360 ml) Memphis BBQ Sauce (page 161)

Preheat the oven to 425°F (220°C). Begin soaking the dates for the Memphis BBQ Sauce (page 161).

To make the buns, rinse the sweet potato well or peel it. Cut it crosswise into ½-inch (1-cm)-thick rounds. Line a metal baking sheet with parchment paper and add the rounds, drizzling with the oil and massaging them on both sides with your hands. Bake for 10 minutes, flip each round over, and bake for 10 more minutes. Set aside.

To make the filling, heat a large sauté pan with straight sides for several minutes over medium heat until hot, and add the avocado oil, swirling to coat the bottom of the pan. Add the ground beef and break it into large pieces. Let it brown undisturbed for about 5 minutes.

Finish making the Memphis BBQ Sauce while the beef is cooking.

Break the beef into smaller crumbles and sprinkle with the salt. Add the onion and bell pepper, stirring about every minute and cooking for about 3 to 5 minutes, until no signs of pink remain and the vegetables have softened. Pour the Memphis BBQ Sauce into the pan with the beef and mix it all together. Allow it to simmer gently for a few minutes to thicken. Serve the Sloppy Joe mixture between 2 sweet potato buns or as open-faced bites. If it's too messy, you can always just eat it with a knife and fork.

Bacon-Wrapped Mini Meatloaves with Carolina Mustard BBQ Sauce

These mini meatloaves are an exciting update to the tired old recipe, using an incredible sweet and tangy mustard BBQ sauce as the topping instead of boring ketchup. To make it Paleo while maintaining a soft texture, I've replaced the breadcrumbs with crushed pork rinds, which are by far my favorite breadcrumb replacement. These babies also freeze extremely well, so consider doubling the batch to freeze some.

🕐 **On the table in less than 45 minutes** | **Yield: 4–6 servings**

2 large eggs

¾ cup (83 g) peeled and shredded carrot (about 1 large carrot)

¼ cup (40 g) finely chopped onion (about ½ small onion)

⅓ cup (18 g) parsley leaves, finely chopped

4 large cloves garlic, minced

1 tbsp (15 ml) apple cider vinegar

1½ tsp (8 g) fine Himalayan salt

½ tsp freshly cracked black pepper

¾ cup (42 g) crushed pork rinds

1½ lbs (680 g) 10-percent-fat ground beef

1 batch of Carolina Mustard BBQ Sauce (page 155)

4 slices of bacon, cut in half crosswise

Preheat the oven to 400°F (200°C).

In a large bowl, whisk the eggs. Mix in the carrot, onion, parsley, garlic, vinegar, salt and pepper. Crush the pork rinds inside the bag they came in using a rolling pin or heavy can. You can also whiz them up in a food processor with an S-blade. Add the powdered pork rinds and ground beef to the mixture in the bowl. Mix everything together using your hands, taking care not to overwork the meat.

Divide the meat mixture into 4 equal-sized pieces. Using a baking sheet, gently form each into a rectangular shape that is not thicker than 1 inch (2.5 cm), about 4 to 5 inches (10 to 13 cm) long and 2 to 3 inches (5 to 8 cm) wide.

Spoon about ½ tablespoon (8 ml) of the BBQ sauce on top of each mini meatloaf (be careful not to contaminate the sauce with raw meat during this step). Use a second spoon to spread the sauce across the top of each mini loaf. Lay 2 of the bacon slice halves on top of each loaf to cover the top. If your bacon is very narrow, you may need an extra half slice to cover each loaf. Finally, spoon another ½ tablespoon (8 ml) or so of sauce on top of the bacon slices. Bake for 25 minutes. Serve with extra mustard BBQ sauce drizzled on top.

MAKE IT A MEAL: Pairs well with Colcannon (page 107) or Smoky Roasted Asparagus (page 97).

Chef's Note: Powdered pork rinds, also known as pork rind breadcrumbs or pork panko, make an excellent substitute in any recipe that calls for, you guessed it, breadcrumbs. They're low-carb, inexpensive and create a great texture! Better than any Paleo-friendly flour, in my opinion.

Caribbean Cottage Pie

Plantains are probably my favorite starch, and they're more versatile than any other. Thankfully they are widely available even in mainstream grocery stores in the U.S. The mashed topping in this recipe is a traditional dish in the Dominican Republic and gives mashed potatoes a run for their money. The filling has Puerto Rican flavoring, and this combo is a unique and delicious take on an old classic.

🕐 **On the table in 45 minutes** | **Yield: 4 servings**

FOR THE MASHED TOPPING

4 green plantains

1 tsp fine Himalayan salt

¼ cup (60 ml) extra-virgin olive oil, ghee or lard

FOR THE FILLING

½ tbsp (8 ml) avocado oil, ghee or lard

1 lb (454 g) ground beef

1 tsp fine Himalayan salt

1 tsp dried oregano

1 small onion, chopped

1 red bell pepper, chopped

4 large cloves garlic, minced

½ bunch cilantro, lower stems removed

2 tbsp (20 g) sliced green olives (about 8 olives)

Juice of 1 lime

Preheat the oven to 375°F (190°C).

To make the topping, bring about 5 cups (1.2 L) of water to a boil (this takes about 10 minutes) in a medium-sized pot. Peel the plantains by slicing the tips off and cutting a slit down the length of the peel. Pull the peel off with your fingers. If the plantains are very difficult to peel, you can cook them without peeling as the peels will come off easily after boiling.

Add the plantains to the boiling water with a pinch of salt and cook until fork-tender, about 20 minutes. Mash them with ½ cup (120 ml) cold water, salt and olive oil for a more rustic texture, or purée in a food processor or blender for a smoother texture.

To make the filling, while the plantains are boiling, heat a large skillet for several minutes over medium heat until hot. Add the oil and swirl to coat the bottom of the pan. Crumble the ground beef into the pan and add the salt and oregano. Cook until the meat is browned, about 10 minutes. Add the onion and bell pepper and cook for about 5 minutes. Add the garlic and cook for 1 minute. Remove the pan from the heat and stir in the cilantro, olives and lime juice.

Pour the filling mixture into the bottom of an 8 x 8–inch (20 x 20–cm) glass baking dish or similarly sized casserole dish or cast-iron pan and spread the plantain topping on top. Bake for 10 to 15 minutes, or until bubbling. Serve immediately.

Time-Saving Tip: If you're really pressed for time, you can skip turning this into a pie and simply serve the meat and mashed plantains separately. However, I strongly recommend making the pie—the presentation is so fun and the flavor improves!

Beet Bolognese with Spaghetti Squash Noodles

This dish is an absolutely veggie-packed alternative to spaghetti. Cooking all of the components from scratch at the same time probably makes this the most "difficult" recipe in the whole book, but it is easy to prep the spaghetti squash and the Beet Marinara (page 164) in advance to make this meal come together easier on a weeknight.

🕐 **On the table in 45 minutes** | **Yield: 6–8 servings**

FOR THE SPAGHETTI SQUASH

1 large spaghetti squash

2 tbsp (30 ml) extra-virgin olive oil

Few pinches of fine Himalayan salt

FOR THE BEET BOLOGNESE

1 batch of Beet Marinara (page 164)

2 tsp (10 ml) avocado oil

2 lbs (907 g) 10-percent-fat ground beef

1 tsp fine Himalayan salt

Chef's Note: To reheat spaghetti squash, cook it in a heated skillet with some extra-virgin olive oil for about 5 to 7 minutes, or until warmed through. The Bolognese can also be reheated in a skillet.

Preheat the oven to 425°F (220°C). If the Beet Marinara isn't pre-made, start cooking it first.

To make the spaghetti squash, rinse the outside of the squash and carefully cut it crosswise into rounds no thicker than 1 inch (2.5 cm). Use a spoon to scoop out the seeds from the center of each round. Place the rounds on a large metal baking sheet, brush both sides of each round with olive oil and season the tops with salt. Bake for 15 minutes. Carefully flip each round over and bake for another 15 minutes, until the strands can easily be pulled away with a fork. Let them cool a few minutes, and then peel away the skin from each round and separate the strands with a fork. Set the strands aside in a bowl and cover to keep warm.

To make the Bolognese, heat a large sauté pan with straight sides for several minutes over medium heat until hot. Add the avocado oil, swirling to coat the bottom of the pan. Add the ground beef and break it into large pieces. Let it brown undisturbed for about 5 minutes.

Break the beef into smaller crumbles and sprinkle with the salt, stirring about every minute and cooking for 3 to 5 minutes more, until no signs of pink remain. Pour the Beet Marinara into the pan with the beef and mix it all together. Allow it to simmer gently for a few minutes, or until the spaghetti squash is done. Serve by putting about 1 cup (124 g) of spaghetti squash into each bowl and topping it with a generous amount of the Bolognese sauce.

SEAFOOD

Don't be intimidated by the seafood counter at the grocery store. Because seafood is some of the fastest-cooking protein out there, it is an excellent choice for busy weeknights or any time you want your meal ready in a jiffy. Even better, canned fish like salmon or tuna is a fabulous "emergency" protein to have on hand for those days when you forget to thaw meat, or your dinner plans fall through and you need something to prevent you from ordering takeout.

← See recipe on page 81.

Pan-Seared Crispy Skin Salmon

This is hands-down my favorite way to cook fresh salmon. I don't know about you, but I find perfectly crispy salmon skin to be addictively delicious, and I would rather not eat salmon than eat a fillet with soggy skin. Thankfully it is so fast and easy to make the crispiest salmon skin by pan-searing your fish. Just make sure to serve your sauce on the side, not on top, or else you'll ruin your effort!

On the table in under 15 minutes | **Yield: 4 servings**

1½ tbsp (23 ml) avocado oil

1 lb (454 g) wild-caught salmon, cut into 4-oz (113-g) fillets

Few pinches of fine Himalayan salt and freshly cracked black pepper

Your favorite sauce from the Sauces chapter (pages 151–165, optional)

Heat a large skillet for several minutes over medium heat until hot. Add the oil and swirl the pan to coat the bottom. It is critical to have a hot pan for crispy skin.

Pat the salmon dry and sprinkle all sides with a few generous pinches of salt and pepper. Add the fillets one at a time to the pan with the skin side down. Use a spatula to gently press the top of each for a few seconds as soon as you add it. This prevents the skin from wrinkling as it rapidly contracts upon contact with the pan. Cook, occasionally pressing down on the fillets to ensure good skin contact with the pan, until the salmon is almost done and the skin releases effortlessly from the pan, about 5 to 7 minutes, depending on the thickness. The fillets are ready to flip when the skin is a lovely golden brown color and the sides of the salmon look cooked with only the top looking raw. Flip the fillets over to briefly sear the tops, cooking for less than 1 minute.

Serve skin-side up and with any sauce on the side to keep the skin nice and crispy. The Comeback Sauce (page 152), Avocado Crema (page 156) and White BBQ Sauce (page 158) are my favorites to serve with this recipe.

MAKE IT A MEAL: Pairs well with Zesty Mojo Red Cabbage Coleslaw (page 90), Roasted Mushrooms with Gremolata (page 108) or Smoky Roasted Asparagus (page 97).

Lemon-Garlic Cod

Wild-caught cod is an affordable white fish that is easy to find at the seafood counter. It has a lovely flaky, creamy texture and is so fast to cook on a busy weeknight. Lemon and garlic are the absolute perfect seasonings for a melt-in-your-mouth meal that feels like a restaurant dish.

On the table in 15 minutes | **Yield: 4 servings**

1 lemon

2–3 cloves garlic, minced

2 tbsp (30 ml) melted ghee or extra-virgin olive oil

½ tsp fine Himalayan salt

½ tsp freshly cracked black pepper

1 lb (454 g) fresh cod

Preheat the oven to 400°F (200°C).

Cut the lemon in half. Squeeze the juice from one half into a small bowl, and cut the other half into round slices that are as thin as possible. Using a mandoline slicer is a great way to do this. Add the garlic, ghee, salt and pepper to the lemon juice to make a sauce.

Cut the cod into 4 (4-oz [113-g]) portions. Lightly grease a 9 x 13–inch (23 x 33–cm) baking dish and place the cod inside. Pour the sauce over the fish and then divide the lemon slices on top. Bake for 10 to 12 minutes, or until the cod easily flakes with a fork. Serve immediately, with the sauce from the baking dish spooned on top of each portion.

MAKE IT A MEAL: Pairs well with Garlicky Mustard Greens (page 96), Fried Ripe Plantains (page 62) or Cheesy Creamed Spinach and Mushrooms (page 103).

Kickin' Salmon Patties with Comeback Sauce

Salmon patties take me back to childhood. I can remember my grandma cooking them up for me when I'd go visit after school because they were one of my favorite dishes. Plus they were fast and easy for her to cook. This is a flourless update of her classic recipe, with a nice kick from the horseradish, mustard and garlic. Canned salmon is a budget-friendly way to incorporate healthy omega-3 rich fish into your diet.

On the table in 20 minutes | **Yield: 2–3 servings**

1 (14.75-oz [417-g]) can pink salmon with skin and bones, well drained

½ cup (28 g) crushed pork rinds

2 tbsp (30 g) prepared horseradish

1 tbsp (15 ml) Dijon mustard

2 large eggs

1 tsp freshly cracked black pepper

½ tsp fine Himalayan salt

4 cloves garlic, minced

⅛–¼ tsp cayenne pepper (optional)

2 tbsp (30 g) lard, ghee or avocado oil

1 batch of Comeback Sauce (page 152)

In a mixing bowl, add the drained salmon, crushed pork rinds, horseradish, mustard, eggs, pepper, salt, garlic and cayenne (if using) and combine. If your prepared horseradish is very liquidy, squeeze out the excess before adding it to the bowl. Leave the bones in the salmon for some extra nutrition. They're safe (and delicious) to eat from canned salmon. Set aside.

Heat a large 12-inch (30-cm) skillet for several minutes over medium heat until hot. Melt the cooking fat, swirling the pan to coat the bottom. While the pan is heating, divide the salmon mixture into 8 to 10 portions, then roll each into a ball between your hands and gently flatten it into a disc shape the size of your palm, about ½ inch (1 cm) thick. Fry the patties for about 5 to 6 minutes per side, until both sides are golden brown and cooked through. They should all just fit into your pan, but if not, cook them in batches.

Serve the patties immediately with the Comeback Sauce. Leftovers can be reheated in a 350°F (180°C) oven for about 10 minutes.

Alternative cooking method: Lightly grease a metal baking sheet with avocado oil and place the patties on it. Brush or spray the tops with additional avocado oil. Bake at 400°F (200°C) for 10 minutes. Carefully flip using a spatula, brush or spray additional oil on top and bake 10 minutes.

MAKE IT A MEAL: Pairs well with steamed broccoli (page 22), Sautéed Radishes with Greens (page 94) or Lemon-Garlic Brussels Sprout Chips (page 99).

Mojo Shrimp Skillet with Cauliflower Rice

Mojo criollo is a beloved Cuban marinade traditionally made from a special type of orange called a sour orange that has a bitter flavor that is perfect for marinades and sauces. Sour oranges are very hard to find outside of south Florida, but thankfully a blend of regular orange and lime juices works amazingly well as a delicious substitute. This dish is what you call a flavor bomb and is an amazing way to make cauliflower rice something you crave eating!

On the table in 20 minutes | **Yield: 3 servings**

FOR THE CAULIFLOWER RICE

1 head cauliflower

1½ tbsp (23 ml) extra-virgin olive oil or melted ghee

½ tsp fine Himalayan salt

FOR THE SHRIMP

½ cup (120 ml) fresh orange juice (about 1–2 navel oranges)

½ cup (120 ml) fresh lime juice (about 3–4 limes)

6 cloves garlic, minced

½ tsp fine Himalayan salt

¼ tsp freshly cracked black pepper

¼ tsp dried oregano

1 tbsp (15 ml) extra-virgin olive oil, plus 2 tsp (10 ml) for cooking

1 lb (454 g) shrimp, peeled, tail removed and deveined (any size)

Chopped cilantro, to garnish

Preheat the oven to 400°F (200°C).

First, prepare the cauliflower rice. Remove the leaves and stem and cut the head into quarters by slicing vertically through the stem. Cut each quarter at an angle to remove the tough inner core from the florets. Place half of the florets into the bowl of a food processor with the S-blade and pulse about a dozen times before whizzing continuously until a rice-like texture is achieved. A 2-pound (907-g) head of cauliflower will yield about 5 cups (930 g) of cauliflower rice. Spread the cauliflower rice on a baking sheet, drizzle with the olive oil and sprinkle the salt on top. Gently toss together with your hands and spread it in an even layer across the sheet. Bake for 5 minutes. Remove and stir briefly (watch out for steam when you open the oven) and cook for 5 minutes.

Meanwhile, prepare the mojo sauce by mixing the orange juice, lime juice, garlic, salt, pepper, oregano and 1 tablespoon (15 ml) of the olive oil together in a bowl. Add the shrimp and let them briefly marinate while you preheat a large skillet over medium heat for several minutes, until hot. Add the remaining oil to coat the heated pan and then remove the shrimp from the marinade and cook for about 1 minute. Pour in the marinade and let it come to a simmer for another 2 to 3 minutes. Remove it from the heat once the shrimp are opaque and cooked through.

Serve the shrimp over a generous portion of Cauliflower Rice with a few spoonfuls of the delicious sauce on top so that the rice can soak it up. Garnish with cilantro.

Coconut Shrimp with Orange Dipping Sauce

Coconut shrimp is a popular menu item at many restaurants, and it really isn't too much trouble to recreate this dish at home with healthy ingredients. The oven-baked version of this recipe is the least fussy and fastest, but pan-frying definitely results in the best crispy and crunchy texture.

On the table in 30 minutes | **Yield: 4 servings**

FOR THE SHRIMP

¼ cup (32 g) tapioca starch

1 egg, well beaten

½ tsp fine Himalayan salt

¼ tsp freshly cracked black pepper

¼ tsp granulated onion

2 cups (186 g) finely shredded unsweetened coconut

1 lb (454 g) raw shrimp, peeled and deveined

1 tbsp (15 ml) avocado oil

FOR THE ORANGE SAUCE

1¼ cups (300 ml) fresh orange juice (about 3 navel oranges)

1 tsp ginger powder

1 tbsp (15 ml) coconut aminos

1 tsp hydrolyzed collagen (see page 168 for more info)

1 large clove garlic, minced

1–2 tsp (5–10 ml) raw honey (optional)

To make the shrimp, place the tapioca starch in a small bowl. Add the egg to a second small bowl and whisk in the salt, pepper and granulated onion. Add the shredded coconut to a third bowl. Dip the shrimp in the tapioca starch, then in the egg mixture and finally press it into the coconut shreds. Set them aside on a large plate in a single layer. Heat a large skillet over medium heat for several minutes until hot. Add the oil and swirl to coat the bottom of the pan. Fry the shrimp in batches, cooking each side for about 2 minutes. Transfer them to a paper towel–lined plate.

While the shrimp are cooking, make the sauce. Add the orange juice, ginger and coconut aminos to a small saucepan over medium-high heat. Bring to a low boil and simmer for about 5 minutes, or until reduced by about half. Stir in the collagen and garlic and cook briefly until fragrant, then remove from the heat. To thicken and sweeten the sauce further, you can stir in 1 to 2 teaspoons (5 to 10 ml) of raw honey.

Alternative cooking method: Preheat the oven to 425°F (220°C). Arrange the breaded shrimp on a metal baking sheet lightly greased with avocado oil. Spray the tops of all the shrimp with avocado oil to make them crispier. Bake for about 10 minutes, or until cooked through. Serve with dipping sauce on the side.

*See photo on page 74.

Chef's Note: Medium to jumbo shrimp are good for this recipe. Total time is based on using shrimp that were purchased peeled and deveined.

MAKE IT A MEAL: Pairs well with Garlicky Mustard Greens (page 96) or steamed broccoli (page 22) (dip it in the sauce!).

Roux-less Shrimp Creole

Shrimp Creole is such a classic dish from Louisiana, and I love how simple it is to cook up after a long day of work. Don't let the long list of seasonings intimidate you. I promise it all comes together quickly. Traditionally, this dish is made with a roux (flour toasted in fat), but you won't miss it one bit amidst all of the spices in this dish. If you're interested in a version with a roux, I do have one on my website that you can try out.

On the table in 30 minutes | **Yield: 4 servings**

2 tbsp (30 ml) ghee or avocado oil

1 medium onion, chopped

1 green bell pepper, chopped

3–4 stalks celery, thinly sliced

1 tsp fine Himalayan salt

½ tsp dried thyme

½ tsp granulated garlic

½ tsp freshly cracked black pepper

¼ tsp white pepper (or more black pepper)

¼ tsp cayenne pepper, or to taste

Pinch of ground cloves

6 cloves garlic, minced

1 (28-oz [794-g]) can chopped tomatoes

½ tbsp (8 ml) coconut aminos

½ tbsp (8 ml) Louisiana-style hot pepper sauce

½ cup (120 ml) water

1 lb (454 g) raw shrimp, peeled, tail removed and deveined

Sliced green onions, to garnish

1 batch of Cauliflower Rice (page 53, optional)

Heat a large skillet for several minutes over medium heat until hot. Add the ghee or oil and swirl it around to coat the pan. Add the onion, bell pepper, celery (also known as "the trinity" or "Cajun trinity"), salt, thyme, granulated garlic, black pepper, white pepper, cayenne and cloves and cook until the trinity has softened, about 10 minutes.

Add the minced garlic and cook for 1 minute. Add the tomatoes, coconut aminos, hot sauce, water and shrimp and bring to a simmer. Cook for about 5 to 7 minutes, or until the shrimp are opaque and cooked through. Taste and adjust the seasonings as needed and serve with a garnish of green onions. This dish can be eaten alone as a kind of stew or served on top of Cauliflower Rice.

Chef's Notes: Total cook time is based on using shrimp that were purchased already peeled, deveined and with the tail removed. Check the freezer section if the fresh counter doesn't have them available.

For the "Cajun trinity" of onions, bell pepper and celery, aim for a ratio of 2 parts onion to 1 part each bell pepper and celery. I like to make double whenever I am making some for a recipe and freeze half to have on hand for a future meal. This strategy is a great way to use up a partial head of celery.

Stovetop Creamy Tuna Casserole

Tuna casserole was one of my favorite meals growing up, but it was made from a box with a bunch of processed and inflammatory ingredients. Thankfully, it is easy to recreate that rich, creamy, comforting blend of flavors with fresh, real food ingredients. Bonus: This recipe is cooked entirely on the stovetop and doesn't require baking in the oven. And I really love using the carrots as ribbons to replace noodles since they give a nice texture and make the dish so pretty.

On the table in 30 minutes | **Yield: 4 servings**

1 tbsp (15 ml) extra-virgin olive oil

1 small onion, chopped

2 stalks celery, thinly sliced

1½ tsp (8 g) fine Himalayan salt

1 tsp dried thyme

½ tsp granulated garlic

½ tsp granulated onion

½ tsp freshly cracked black pepper

8 oz (226 g) cremini mushrooms, sliced

4 cloves garlic, minced

1½ tbsp (12 g) nutritional yeast

¾ cup (180 ml) chicken broth

Juice of 1 lime

8 oz (226 g) carrots, cut into ribbons with a vegetable peeler

2 (5-oz [142-g]) cans albacore tuna, drained

2 tbsp (30 ml) canned full-fat coconut milk (optional)

2 green onions, sliced, to garnish

Heat a large skillet for several minutes over medium heat until hot. Add the oil and swirl it around to coat the pan. Add the onion, celery, salt, thyme, granulated garlic and onion, and pepper and sauté for 6 to 7 minutes. Add the mushrooms, garlic and nutritional yeast and cook for 3 to 4 minutes to soften the mushrooms.

Add the chicken broth, lime juice, carrot ribbons and drained tuna, making sure to break up the tuna into small flakes. Let it come to a bubble and cook for 5 to 7 minutes to soften the carrot ribbons and allow all the flavors to meld. Stir in the coconut milk (if using) toward the end of cooking. Garnish with the green onions and serve immediately.

VEGETABLES

I sure love cooking with vegetables—can you tell? It's a sign of my Southern roots. While there are 19 stand-alone veggie recipes in this chapter, there are more than 30 vegetable sides when you count those scattered throughout this book that are built in with main dishes. I knew when I was planning out this book that I didn't want any vegetable to be an afterthought. I wanted vegetables to be prominent. I wanted to empower you to know how to best cook a huge variety of commonly available vegetables into delicious dishes that your family will actually want to eat. I can't tell you how many times I've cooked for friends and served them a vegetable they told me they didn't think they liked, but after eating mine, said they loved it. It all comes down to proper cooking methods and the right seasonings, and after working through this chapter you'll have both things down pat. The best part? Vegetables are fast and easy to cook! I've carefully curated these recipes to be quick for weeknight meals.

Vegetables provide so many important nutrients on a Paleo diet, including fiber. If you've set a goal to eat more veggies this year, this chapter should make that easy for you!

← See recipe on page 90.

Warm Lemon-Dill Cucumbers

The first time I sautéed a cucumber, it was an accident. I thought it was a zucchini one morning many years ago when I was probably too sleepy to be cooking yet. I was pleasantly surprised that it actually tasted really good! That fateful morning I had cooked cucumber with garlic, but I much prefer this combo of fresh lemon juice and dill for a crisp, clean, cool flavor combination that's perfect for summer weather, when cucumbers are plentiful. If you find raw cucumbers difficult on your tummy, then you'll love how much easier to digest they are when cooked.

On the table in 10 minutes | **Yield: 4 servings**

1 tbsp (15 ml) extra-virgin olive oil or avocado oil

1 lb (454 g) cucumbers, cut into thin coins or half moons

½ tsp fine Himalayan salt, or to taste

¼ lemon, cut into wedges

1 tbsp (4 g) fresh chopped dill fronds

Heat a large skillet over medium heat for several minutes until hot. Add the oil and swirl to coat the pan. Remove the skin from the cucumbers with a vegetable peeler if desired.

Sauté the cucumbers with the salt for about 5 to 7 minutes, or until they are tender and slightly browning in a few places. Do not overcook or fully brown them because the texture will become unpleasantly mushy. Transfer the cucumbers to a serving bowl and squeeze a wedge or two of lemon juice over top and toss with the dill. Taste and add more lemon juice or salt, if needed. Serve immediately. This dish is best served fresh, since reheated cucumbers will take on a mushy consistency.

Chef's Note: I recommend peeling grocery store cucumbers since they are coated heavily with wax, but if you grow your own or get them from a farmers market, I suggest keeping the skin on.

Zesty Mojo Red Cabbage Coleslaw

I've never been a big fan of mayonnaise-based coleslaw, but I absolutely love this garlicky-citrus version made with bright and beautiful red cabbage. It is a feast for the eyes as well as the taste buds! This makes a huge batch of slaw to feed a crowd or for batch cooking.

 On the table in 15 minutes | **Yield: 6–8 servings**

FOR THE COLESLAW

6 cups (420 g) shredded red cabbage (about 1 small head)

1 cup (110 g) peeled and shredded carrots (about 3 carrots)

½ packed cup (10 g) chopped cilantro

1 large shallot, minced

FOR THE MOJO DRESSING

¼ cup (60 ml) freshly squeezed orange juice

¼ cup (60 ml) freshly squeezed lime juice

2–3 large cloves garlic, minced

½ tsp fine Himalayan salt

¼ tsp dried oregano

⅛ tsp freshly cracked black pepper

2 tbsp (30 ml) extra-virgin olive oil

To make the slaw, add the cabbage, carrots, cilantro and shallot to a large bowl and mix.

To make the dressing, add the orange juice, lime juice, garlic, salt, oregano, pepper and olive oil to a small bowl and whisk vigorously. Pour the dressing over the slaw and massage into the vegetables for about 2 minutes to soften them and make them easier to digest. You can serve it immediately or allow it to chill in the fridge to serve later.

Time-Saving Tip: You can certainly use a pre-packaged bag of slaw mix from the grocery store if you're really strapped for time. Just add the cilantro and shallot to it and massage in the dressing and you're done!

Chef's Note: To shred the cabbage, first cut it in half from stem to top. Then cut into quarters and use a diagonal slice to remove the tough inner core from each wedge. Either use a food processor, box grater, or your knife to shred.

Sautéed Zucchini Coins with Basil

This recipe teaches you all the tricks you need to know to prevent sautéed zucchini from turning out mushy. Use a hot pan, plenty of fat, thicker slices, don't move them while they're cooking and don't crowd them in the pan. This is such a simple dish, using two summer staples, but it is bursting with flavor and will turn you into a zucchini lover. Just say no to mushy summer squash!

🕐 **On the table in 15 minutes** | **Yield: 4 servings**

1 tbsp (15 ml) extra-virgin olive oil

1 lb (454 g) zucchini, sliced into ½–¾" (1–2-cm) coins

Few pinches of fine Himalayan salt and freshly cracked black pepper

2 cloves garlic, minced

7 or 8 large basil leaves, chiffonade cut

Heat a large skillet for several minutes over medium heat until hot. Add the oil and swirl the pan to coat the bottom. Season the zucchini coins on both sides with salt and pepper. Add them to the pan in a single layer and let them cook undisturbed for about 2 to 4 minutes. The bottoms should be nicely browned and they should not stick to the pan when you try to flip them. Flip the coins and cook for 2 to 4 minutes, until the zucchini is fork tender and browned. Add the garlic toward the very end and cook for about a minute.

Transfer the zucchini and garlic to a serving dish and toss with the basil. Serve immediately. Heating up leftovers is not recommended as the texture will become mushy.

Chef's Notes: You can use this method to cook any summer squash. I recommend going to your local farmers market to see what varieties they are growing. Zephyr squash is one of my favorites, if you can find it!

To perform a chiffonade cut for the basil leaves, stack the leaves on top of each other and then roll them up from stem to leaf tip. Cut the roll crosswise into thin strips.

Sautéed Radishes with Greens

Did you know that the nutritional value of radish greens exceeds that of the roots? The greens are an excellent source of calcium and have double the amount of vitamin C of the radishes themselves. The leaves also have double the phenolic compounds and quadruple the flavonoids of the roots. It makes sense when you remember that radishes are a type of Brassica, like kale, broccoli, etc. I love cooking radishes with their greens right in the same pan. It's easy, fast, delicious and stretches the food further. I hope you'll never toss another bunch of radish greens again after trying this recipe.

🕐 **On the table in 15 minutes** | **Yield: 2 servings**

8–10 radishes with greens (about 1 bunch)

1 tbsp (15 ml) extra-virgin olive oil, ghee or avocado oil

¼ heaping tsp dried thyme or rosemary

2 large cloves garlic, minced

½ tsp fine Himalayan salt

¼ tsp freshly cracked black pepper

Cut the greens off each radish and rinse well. Wash the roots well under running water, scrubbing to remove any soil. Remove the root tip from each radish and discard (composting is great!). Slice each root in half from root tip to top, then cut crosswise into thin half-moons. Coarsely chop the greens.

Heat a large skillet for several minutes over medium heat until hot. Add the oil and swirl to coat the bottom of the pan. Sauté the roots for 6 to 8 minutes, or until they begin to turn translucent and become soft. Add the thyme, garlic, salt and black pepper and cook 1 to 2 minutes. Add the chopped greens and cook until they are wilted down, about 1 to 2 minutes. Serve as a side dish to any meal. This makes an especially tasty breakfast side dish.

Chef's Note: If the greens look very wilted or discolored, don't cook them. Young, fresh, tender greens taste the best and have the best texture.

Garlicky Mustard Greens

Where I come from in Georgia, most people like to boil greens like mustard for a long time, usually with bacon and onion. I certainly enjoy eating them like that, especially in the winter, but most days I prefer this method since it is so fast and requires only minimal ingredients for a delicious and flavor-packed side.

 On the table in less than 15 minutes | Yield: 4 servings

2 tbsp (30 ml) extra-virgin olive oil

4–6 cloves garlic, minced

¼ tsp fine Himalayan salt, or more to taste

1 lb (454 g) mustard greens, rinsed well and chopped into thin slices

Heat a large sauté pan with straight sides over medium heat for several minutes until hot. Add the oil and swirl to coat the bottom of the pan. Add the garlic and salt and sauté until the garlic is nice and fragrant, about a minute. Add the mustard greens and sauté them, stirring frequently, until they are tender, about 5 to 7 minutes. Add a splash or two of water while they cook to encourage them to wilt down, if needed. Serve immediately.

Chef's Note: Depending on the type, size and age of the mustard greens, the stems may be very tender (young, small leaves) or they may be a little tough and woody (larger, mature leaves). There is no reason to cut out and discard tender stems. Test them by cutting a small piece from the very bottom and biting into it raw. If it is easy to chew, then you should leave it. If it feels fibrous and chewy, it is best to cut off the lower part of each stem.

Smoky Roasted Asparagus

Asparagus is an underrated vegetable in my opinion. It is so easy to prepare and can be dressed up so many different ways to complement its delightful nutty, grassy flavor and tender texture. I absolutely love cooking it with garlic and smoked paprika and think you will, too!

 On the table in a little over 15 minutes | Yield: 2–4 servings

1 lb (454 g) asparagus, rinsed and dried

2 tsp (10 ml) extra-virgin olive oil or avocado oil

½ tsp smoked paprika

¼ tsp fine Himalayan salt

¼ tsp freshly cracked black pepper

¼ tsp granulated garlic

Lemon wedges, for serving (optional)

Heat the oven to 400°F (200°C).

Snap the woody stem off the lower portion of each stalk of asparagus. If you bend the lower portion of the stalk it will snap off exactly where it needs to. Or, you can just use a knife to cut the bottom inch or so off all together.

Place the trimmed asparagus on a metal baking sheet, drizzle the oil over the stalks and then sprinkle the paprika, salt, pepper and garlic on top. Use your hands to massage the oil and seasonings over every stalk. Bake for 10 to 15 minutes depending on the thickness of the stalks, which can vary significantly. Sometimes asparagus is pencil thin, and other times it can be as thick as your thumb. The asparagus is done when it's easily pierced with a fork and lightly browned. Serve with lemon wedges to squeeze over the asparagus, if desired.

Lemon-Garlic Brussels Sprout Chips

Brussels sprout chips blow kale chips out of the water and are something my husband and I will fight over whenever I make a batch. The prep work is faster and easier, they're less finicky while roasting and overall the flavor is better thanks to the natural nuttiness of Brussels sprouts. Bonus: Peeling off the outer leaves makes the sprouts roast better, anyway, and turns what would have been just one side dish into two, stretching your food budget further.

🕐 **On the table in 15 minutes** | **Yield: 2 servings as a side or 4 as a snack**

1 lb (454 g) Brussels sprouts

1 tbsp (15 ml) extra-virgin olive oil, avocado oil or melted ghee

½ tsp granulated garlic

Few pinches of fine Himalayan salt and freshly cracked black pepper

½ tbsp (6 g) finely grated lemon zest

Preheat the oven to 350°F (180°C).

Peel the loose outer leaves from each sprout, around 4 to 8 from each one. Place the Brussels sprout leaves on a large baking sheet in a single layer and drizzle with the oil. Then gently massage the leaves with your hands to coat them well with the oil. Sprinkle the garlic, salt and pepper on top and gently toss the leaves with your hands. Spread them out into a single layer.

Bake for 8 to 10 minutes, or until they are crispy with some browned edges. To make them extra crispy, turn the broiler on high for 1 to 2 minutes, but watch them very closely to make sure they do not burn. Zest the lemon over the chips and serve them immediately as a snack or small side.

Chef's Note: Save the peeled sprouts to cook later using the recipe for Crispy Roasted Brussels Sprouts with White BBQ Sauce (page 115).

Ethiopian Cabbage

Cabbage is such an affordable, healthy vegetable, and it also happens to be on the Environmental Working Group's Clean Fifteen produce list, meaning it is one of the least pesticide-contaminated vegetables grown conventionally. This is one of my favorite ways to cook the humble cabbage because I love the warm flavor of turmeric. Some recipes call for adding carrots and potatoes to the cabbage for this dish, but I prefer to cook it alone, and this is how my favorite Ethiopian restaurant serves it, too.

🕐 **On the table in 15 minutes** | **Yield: 4 servings**

2–3 tbsp (30–45 ml) extra-virgin olive oil

1 small white onion, thinly sliced into half moons

4 cloves garlic, minced

2 tsp (10 g) minced fresh ginger

1 small head green cabbage, cored and thinly sliced (about 5–6 cups [350–420 g])

1 tsp fine Himalayan salt

1 tsp turmeric powder

½ tsp freshly cracked black pepper

¼ tsp ground cumin

¼ tsp smoked paprika (optional)

Heat a large 12-inch (30.5-cm) sauté pan with straight sides over medium heat for several minutes until hot. Add the oil and swirl the pan to coat the bottom.

Sauté the onion for about 2 minutes. Add the garlic and ginger and cook briefly until fragrant, less than 1 minute. Add the cabbage, salt, turmeric, pepper, cumin and paprika (if using) and cook, stirring and flipping occasionally, until the cabbage is tender, about 7 to 8 minutes. If the pan seems to be getting dry, add a little extra oil. Serve immediately.

Cheesy Creamed Spinach and Mushrooms

This steakhouse classic gets a healthy makeover with vitamin B-packed nutritional yeast and coconut milk. This recipe will turn anyone into a spinach lover! You can also make this sauce with kale or other dark leafy greens, too.

🕐 **On the table in 15 minutes** | **Yield: 4 servings**

FOR THE SPINACH

½ tbsp (8 ml) extra-virgin olive oil or avocado oil

4 oz (113 g) cremini or baby bella mushrooms, sliced

2 cloves garlic, minced

1 lb (454 g) spinach (baby or mature), rinsed

FOR THE CHEESY SAUCE

¾ cup (180 ml) canned full-fat coconut milk

2 cloves garlic, minced

1 tbsp (8 g) nutritional yeast

½ tsp fine Himalayan salt

¼ tsp freshly cracked black pepper

Pinch of ground nutmeg (optional)

1 tsp gelatin

Heat a sauté pan with straight sides or even a wide-bottomed pot for several minutes over medium heat until hot. Add the oil and swirl the pan to coat the bottom. Add the mushrooms and cook until they have softened and released some liquid, about 5 minutes. Add the garlic and cook for 1 minute. Add the spinach. It's best if the spinach still has some water on it from being rinsed, as this helps it wilt. Use tongs or a spatula to turn the spinach over so that it wilts, cooking for about 2 minutes.

To make the sauce, add the coconut milk, garlic, nutritional yeast, salt, pepper and nutmeg (if using) to a small saucepan and whisk to combine. Add the gelatin by slowly sprinkling it on top so that it can bloom (absorb liquid). This helps prevent it from forming clumps. Heat the mixture over medium heat until it's simmering, whisking occasionally to ensure the gelatin is completely dissolved. Reduce the heat to maintain a gentle simmer.

Transfer the cooked spinach mixture to a serving bowl using tongs so that the cooking liquid is left behind in the pan. Pour the sauce over top and toss to combine. Serve immediately.

Spiced Beet Greens

I know that, sadly, many beet greens end up in the trash because folks either don't know how to cook them or they never realize that they taste delicious. They are also quite nutritious, being an excellent source of many important vitamins and minerals like B2, copper, manganese, potassium, magnesium and calcium. They have a distinctive earthy flavor that is enhanced with the warm spices in this dish. A generous splash of acid at the end of cooking balances all the flavors and is actually a good thing to do to brighten and balance the flavor of any type of cooked greens.

🕐 **On the table in 15 minutes** | **Yield: 2 servings**

2 bunches of beet greens (about 1¼ lbs [567 g])

1 tbsp (15 ml) extra-virgin olive oil

1 medium onion, chopped

1 tsp fine Himalayan salt, or to taste

½ tsp freshly cracked black pepper

¼ tsp paprika

¼ tsp ground cumin

About 1 tbsp (15 ml) fresh lemon or lime juice

Cut the greens off the beets and thoroughly rinse them as they tend to have sand on them.

Heat a large skillet over medium heat for several minutes until hot. Add the oil and swirl the pan to coat the bottom. While the pan is heating, cut the lower stems off where they attach to the greens. Thinly slice the stems and stack the greens and roughly chop them, keeping them separate from the stems. Sauté the stems and onion together for 5 minutes. Add the greens to the pan along with the salt, pepper, paprika and cumin. Use a spatula or tongs to lift and turn the greens to mix them with the stems and onions. Cook them briefly until tender, about 2 minutes. Finish by squeezing the fresh lemon or lime juice into the greens.

Chef's Notes: I encourage you to explore other seasonings when you cook beet greens, or try them simply made with salt, pepper and a little lemon juice.

At grocery stores and farmers markets alike, beet greens are typically sold attached to beets, so save the beets and use them for Beet Marinara (page 164), Brisk Borscht (page 134) or Herbed Beet and Turnip Wedges (page 123).

Colcannon

Colcannon is a traditional Irish and Scottish dish that combines two staples from the region: potatoes and cabbage. Some call it "Irish mashed potatoes." While it may seem strange to intentionally mix greens into mashed potatoes, I promise you'll enjoy it! And if you need an alternative to avoid nightshades, read the substitution notes for options. While cabbage is the traditional green, you can use any leafy green you prefer. Using a dark green like kale provides more visual contrast in the finished dish.

On the table in 25 minutes | Yield: 4 servings

FOR THE POTATOES

3 lbs (1.4 kg) russet potatoes, peeled and coarsely chopped

1 tbsp (18 g) salt, for the cooking water

½ cup (120 ml) chicken bone broth

FOR THE GREENS

6 oz (170 g) bacon, cut into 1" (2.5-cm) pieces

1 small onion, chopped

1 small head green cabbage, coarsely chopped (about 5–6 cups [350–420 g])

1 tsp salt, or to taste

Freshly cracked black pepper, to taste

Cook the potatoes and greens simultaneously.

To make the potatoes, place them in a stockpot and cover them with at least 1 inch (2.5 cm) of water. Salt the water and bring it to a boil over high heat, and then cover and reduce to a low boil for 10 to 15 minutes, or until they are fork tender. Drain in a colander, and then return the potatoes to the hot pot and place it back on the same burner but with the heat turned off. Let them release steam for a few minutes, and then mash them with the broth.

To make the greens, place the bacon in a large skillet and turn on the heat to medium heat. Cook until just crispy, anywhere from 8 to 15 minutes, depending on the bacon. Drain off all but about 1 tablespoon (15 ml) of the rendered bacon fat, and add the onion and cook briefly, about 1 to 2 minutes. Add the cabbage, salt and pepper and cook, stirring occasionally, until softened, about 5 to 7 minutes.

Transfer the mashed potatoes to a serving bowl and fold the greens, onions and most of the bacon into the mashed potatoes, reserving a little bacon to crumble and sprinkle on top as a garnish.

Substitutions: You can use white-fleshed sweet potatoes or peeled turnips in place of the potatoes for a nightshade-free version. If you're using turnips that have greens attached, you can use the greens instead of cabbage. Also, you can use any leafy green you like in place of the cabbage, like kale or collards.

Roasted Mushrooms with Gremolata

Gremolata is a traditional Italian herb condiment that is related to pesto, pistou, persillade and chimichurri. I love the simplicity of gremolata compared to all the others (even though they are all delicious and worthy of exploration). You just need three ingredients to make gremolata, and it can be used in so many ways beyond this recipe. Use it as a topping for steak, pork chops or grilled chicken breast, or use it to give life and brightness to simple sautéed greens or roasted asparagus. Paired with these roasted mushrooms, you will feel like you're eating a dish from a fine restaurant.

🕐 **On the table in 25 minutes** | **Yield: 8 servings**

FOR THE ROASTED MUSHROOMS

1½ lbs (680 g) baby portobello mushrooms, cleaned and sliced

3 tbsp (45 ml) extra-virgin olive oil or avocado oil

Few generous pinches of fine Himalayan salt

FOR THE GREMOLATA

2 cloves garlic, minced

2 tbsp (8 g) chopped parsley leaves (about ¼ bunch)

½ tbsp (7 g) finely grated lemon zest

Pinch of fine Himalayan salt and freshly cracked black pepper

Preheat the oven to 400°F (200°C).

To cook the mushrooms, wipe them gently with a damp cloth to remove any dirt. Cut off the tips of the stems if they are dried out or discolored. Place the sliced mushrooms on 2 metal baking sheets, drizzle them with the oil and season them with salt. Use your hands to gently massage the oil on all surfaces of each mushroom. Spread the mushrooms out so that there is space in between them. If they are too close together on the pan, the moisture will pool around them instead of evaporating and they'll take much longer to cook. Bake for 10 to 12 minutes with one pan on the middle rack and one near the bottom, switching the positions of the sheet pans about halfway through cooking.

To make the gremolata, add the garlic, parsley, lemon zest, salt and pepper to a small bowl and stir together.

Once the mushrooms have finished cooking, add them to a serving bowl and sprinkle the gremolata on top. Gently stir it all together. Taste and add salt and pepper, if necessary. Serve immediately.

Chef's Note: Use these mushrooms as a super flavorful topping for a meatza (page 65). Leftovers are especially good for this.

Irish Carrot Parsnip Mash

My first cookbook, *Latin American Paleo Cooking*, featured many recipes passed down in my Puerto Rican husband's family. For this book, I wanted to explore a few traditional dishes from Ireland, which is where many of my ancestors come from. Parsnips are an underutilized vegetable with a beautifully bright flavor, and they can work well as a substitute for potatoes. The taste is similar to carrots, but stronger and more pungent. Mashing parsnips together with carrots results in a visually beautiful side dish with a unique flavor that will liven up any meal.

🕐 **On the table in less than 30 minutes** | **Yield: 4 servings**

¾ lb (340 g) carrots (about 4 medium carrots), peeled and cut into ½" (1-cm) coins

1 lb (454 g) parsnips (about 4 large parsnips), peeled and cut into ½" (1-cm) coins

2–3 tbsp (30–45 ml) extra-virgin olive oil, avocado oil or ghee

Fine Himalayan salt and white pepper, to taste

Chopped fresh parsley, to garnish

Add the carrots to a medium pot and cover them with at least 1 inch (2.5 cm) of water. Bring to a boil over high heat, and then cover and reduce to a low boil for 10 minutes. Carrots take longer to cook, so they need this head start. Add the parsnips to the pot with the carrots and cook for 10 minutes, until everything is fork tender.

Drain in a colander and return the cooked roots to the pot. Add your fat of choice and use a potato masher to make a coarse mash. Season with salt and pepper to taste. White pepper is preferred to avoid black specks in the final dish. If you prefer a smoother, less-traditional texture, use a food processor with an S-blade attachment to make a purée. Garnish with the parsley to have the three colors of the Irish flag represented in the dish.

Chef's Note: While butter is not Paleo, it is the traditional fat used in this mash, and it's delicious! If you include butter, I recommend trying a good grass-fed Irish butter in this dish.

Sautéed Kale or Collards with Tahini Sauce

When I asked my readers which vegetables they needed help with, I heard from so many that dark leafy greens like kale and collards give them the most trouble. This cooking method can be used for any leafy green (think: chard, mustard greens, beet greens, etc.), and will result in delicious greens that technically don't even need the sauce. But trust me, you will want to use the sauce!

🕐 **On the table in less than 30 minutes** | **Yield: 4 servings**

FOR THE KALE

1 lb (454 g) kale (any variety) or collard greens, rinsed well

2 tbsp (30 ml) extra-virgin olive oil

1 small onion, chopped

3 cloves garlic, minced

1 tbsp (14 g) minced fresh ginger

½ tsp fine Himalayan salt, or to taste

FOR THE TAHINI SAUCE

¼ cup (65 g) tahini

2½ tbsp (38 ml) freshly squeezed lime juice (about 2 limes)

2 tbsp (30 ml) water

1 tbsp (15 ml) coconut aminos

1 tbsp (15 ml) toasted sesame oil

½ tsp fine Himalayan salt

1 clove garlic, minced

½ tbsp (7 g) minced fresh ginger

1–2 tsp (3–6 g) toasted sesame seeds, to garnish

To make the kale, remove the tough ribs by either tearing the leaves away with your hands, or using a knife to cut them out with a v-shaped cut. Discard (or better yet, compost) the ribs. Stack the kale leaves and roughly chop them into pieces about ½ inch (1 cm) thick. Heat a large skillet over medium heat for several minutes until hot. Add the olive oil and swirl to coat the bottom of the pan. Add the onion and cook for about 5 minutes, until the onion starts to get tender. Add the garlic, ginger and salt and cook for 1 minute. Add the kale gradually and use a spatula or tongs to lift and turn the kale to mix it with the onions. As it begins to wilt, add the remaining kale and continue tossing it in the pan for 2 to 3 minutes, or until the leaves are tender and have turned a brighter, vibrant green.

While the onions and kale cook, make the sauce by stirring together the tahini, lime juice, water, coconut aminos, toasted sesame oil, salt, garlic and ginger in a bowl. Taste and adjust the seasonings as desired. Remove the pan from the stovetop and pour the sauce over the kale and toss to combine. You can reserve a small amount of the sauce to use as a topping on each serving. Serve with a garnish of toasted sesame seeds.

> **Chef's Note:** To make toasted sesame seeds, simply heat them in a dry pan over medium heat for about 3 to 5 minutes, stirring frequently to avoid burning. They will brown and become fragrant as they toast.

Crispy Roasted Brussels Sprouts with White BBQ Sauce

Brussels sprouts that have been roasted until crispy are truly one of my favorite foods. They have a delightful nutty flavor that is delicious all on its own, but paired with tangy, creamy White BBQ Sauce (page 158) they are just divine. If you like an extra kick, you can add some extra prepared horseradish to the sauce that you serve with these.

🕐 **On the table in less than 30 minutes | Yield: 2–3 servings**

1 lb (454 g) Brussels sprouts

1 tbsp (15 ml) extra-virgin olive oil or avocado oil

Fine Himalayan salt, to taste

2–3 tbsp (30–45 ml) White BBQ Sauce (page 158)

Preheat the oven to 425°F (220°C).

Remove the loose outer leaves from each sprout and reserve them for making Lemon-Garlic Brussels Sprout Chips (page 99). Cut off and discard the stems and slice the sprouts in half lengthwise, adding any leaves that fall off to the others.

Place the sprouts on a metal baking sheet, drizzle with the oil and season with a few generous pinches of salt. Toss with your hands, making sure the sprouts are coated with the oil, and arrange them in a single layer with the cut side facing down. Bake for 8 to 10 minutes. Then stir the pan and bake for 5 to 7 minutes, or until they are golden brown and crisp. If you want them to be extra crispy, increase the oven temperature to broil and cook an additional 2 to 3 minutes, stirring the sprouts about halfway through to prevent burning.

Drizzle with the White BBQ Sauce.

> **Chef's Note:** You'll only need a few tablespoons of the sauce drizzled on top, so I recommend planning to make a batch of Baked BBQ Chicken Thighs Three Ways (page 38) with the rest of the sauce soon.

Roasted Carrot Fries with Carrot Top Chimichurri

Carrot greens are such a neglected vegetable. Did you know that they are very similar to parsley, and in fact are closely related? That makes them wonderful to use in a chimichurri, which is traditionally made from parsley and used as a condiment for steak in South America. When you can find a bunch of carrots with the greens intact, grab them up so that you can make this bright, fresh, herbaceous sauce that pairs perfectly with roasted carrot fries! Serve it with a steak so that you can use some of the chimichurri there, too.

🕐 **On the table in 30 minutes** | **Yield: 2–3 servings**

FOR THE CARROT FRIES

6–7 medium carrots (about 1 bunch)

1 tsp extra-virgin olive oil

¼ tsp fine Himalayan salt

Freshly cracked black pepper, to taste

FOR THE CHIMICHURRI

1 cup (60 g) chopped carrot greens, thick stems removed (about 1 bunch)

½ cup (120 ml) extra-virgin olive oil

2 tbsp (30 ml) red wine vinegar or coconut vinegar

1 tsp fine Himalayan salt, or to taste

1 tbsp (9 g) minced garlic

½ tsp red pepper flakes (optional)

Preheat the oven to 400°F (200°C).

To make the fries, cut the tops off the carrots and set them aside for the chimichurri. Peel the carrots and cut them in half crosswise. Take the bottom, thin halves and cut them in half lengthwise. Take the top, thick halves and cut them lengthwise into quarters. This will give you spears that are about the same size. Place the carrot spears on a metal baking sheet and drizzle with the oil. Sprinkle the salt and pepper on top. Use your hands to rub the oil and seasonings onto every carrot spear. Spread them evenly on the baking sheet, ensuring they aren't crowded. Roast the carrot spears for 15 to 20 minutes, turning them halfway through cooking.

While the carrots are roasting, make the chimichurri. Massage the carrot greens, olive oil, vinegar and salt together with your hands in a bowl until the greens release some of their water and they soften. Stir in the garlic and pepper flakes (if using). Serve the carrot fries with the chimichurri on the side as a dipping sauce, or spread it on top of each serving.

Chef's Note: If you can't find carrots with the greens attached, you can substitute flat leaf (Italian) parsley in the chimichurri.

Golden Roasted Cauliflower

Isn't it funny how cauliflower has turned into the Paleo and low-carb alternative for SO many things? Pizza, rice, potatoes . . . heck, I've even seen things like pretzels made out of cauliflower flour in stores. That's all cool, but I've been a cauliflower lover since before its superpower to replace so many things was discovered. It is incredibly delicious when roasted with some good seasonings. This seasoning blend is inspired by the ingredients of the traditional Ayurvedic anti-inflammatory drink "golden milk." Warm and spicy, this blend brings out the natural nuttiness of the cauliflower that roasting enhances.

🕐 **On the table in 30 minutes** | **Yield: 4–6 servings**

1 head cauliflower (around 2½ lbs [1.1 kg])

¼ cup (60 ml) extra-virgin olive oil

1½ tsp (3 g) turmeric powder

1½ tsp (4 g) granulated garlic

½ tsp ginger powder

½ tsp freshly cracked black pepper

½ tsp fine Himalayan salt

Preheat the oven to 425°F (220°C).

Cut the cauliflower into florets. First, cut it in half with the knife running from the stem to the top, then, cut it into quarters. Next, cut it at an angle behind the remaining stem. The florets will fall away and you can use your hands to pull them apart into smaller pieces or cut them with the knife. Try to get them all to a similar size so they roast evenly. Place the florets on a metal baking sheet.

In a small bowl, mix together the oil, turmeric, garlic, ginger, pepper and salt until you make a paste. Spoon or brush the paste over the cauliflower florets, tossing to coat them evenly. Arrange them in a single layer without overcrowding them. It's better to split them between 2 baking sheets if in doubt. Roast for 10 minutes. Remove them from the oven and stir with a spatula, and then return them to the oven and cook for 8 to 10 minutes, or until fork tender and nicely browned. Be careful when opening the oven as it may be steamy inside. Serve immediately.

Crispy Baked Rosemary Garlic Steak Fries

These thick-cut steak fries are the perfect weeknight starchy side dish since they are so easy to make in the oven. I really do think they turn out better than deep fried, too, since they aren't so heavy and greasy, just super tender and creamy on the inside and crispy on the outside. This cooking method works for sweet potatoes, too, if you need to swap them out to avoid nightshades.

🕐 **On the table in 30 minutes** | **Yield: 4 servings**

2 lbs (907 g) russet potatoes or sweet potatoes

3 tbsp (45 ml) extra-virgin olive oil, lard or ghee

1 tsp fine Himalayan salt

1 tsp crushed dried rosemary

½ tsp smoked paprika

½ tsp granulated garlic

Preheat the oven to 425°F (220°C).

Either peel the potatoes or scrub them well under running water to remove any soil. Cut each potato in half lengthwise, and then cut each half into about 4 wedges by cutting lengthwise at an angle towards the center. Place the wedges on a metal baking sheet, drizzle with the oil and sprinkle the salt, rosemary, paprika and garlic on top. Toss everything with your hands, ensuring that every wedge has oil on all sides.

Bake on a rack in the middle of the oven for 12 minutes. Use a spatula to carefully flip the fries over to ensure even browning on both sides, and then bake for 10 to 15 minutes, or until they are golden on the outside and tender on the inside.

Chef's Note: Sweet potato fries cook more quickly than russet potatoes, so check them after about 7 minutes of cooking in the second bake to make sure they don't burn.

Herbed Beet and Turnip Wedges

Beets and turnips are two of my favorite root vegetables, and they pair well together in this dish. Roasting them unlocks their full flavor potential and makes them tender on the inside and caramelized on the outside. Bonus: This cooking method means you don't have to peel the roots, saving you prep time. You can also make this recipe with all beets or all turnips—it's up to you! When it comes to root vegetables, I prefer to use an animal fat like fresh lard, ghee or even duck fat because it really brings out the flavors and makes them much heartier and more comforting.

🕐 **On the table in less than 45 minutes** | **Yield: 6–8 servings**

2½ lbs (1.1 kg) beets (any variety) and/ or purple-top turnips

2 tbsp (30 ml) melted lard, extra-virgin olive oil or melted ghee

1 tsp dried thyme

1 tsp fine Himalayan salt

½ tsp freshly cracked black pepper

Preheat the oven to 425°F (220°C).

Thoroughly rinse and scrub the outsides of the beets and turnips to remove any soil. I use a textured dishrag, but you can also use a produce brush. Cut each root in half, and then cut each half into 4 to 6 wedges by aiming your knife diagonally toward the center of the half. The wedges should be 1 inch (2.5 cm) thick or less, so larger roots will need to be cut into more wedges.

Place the wedges on a metal baking sheet, drizzle them with the melted fat and sprinkle the thyme, salt and pepper on top. Use your hands to toss it all together to ensure that every wedge is covered in fat. Arrange the coated wedges in a single layer on the sheet. Bake for 12 minutes. Use a spatula to carefully flip them all over to the other side. Do the best you can. It just helps both sides get that pretty, caramelized crust. Bake for 12 to 15 minutes until they are sizzling, tender and nicely browned. Serve immediately.

SOUPS AND STEWS

Soups don't have to simmer away for hours and hours in order to be delicious and cooked to perfection. These recipes are all bold, flavorful and on your table in anywhere from 10 to 45 minutes, making them versatile for any time you want a warm, comforting meal in a bowl. Tricks like using affordable and fast-cooking ground meat and shredded vegetables drastically decreases the cooking time without sacrificing flavor.

← See recipe on page 133.

Egg Drop Soup

If you've never made your own egg drop soup, you have been missing out. This takeout classic is so easy to make at home and tastes way better than what you get at most restaurants. When you need a comforting, soothing meal in a pinch, make some! Whether you only want to make one serving, or want to feed a dinner party, it's easy to adjust the recipe. Just remember that you'll want one egg per cup (240 ml) of broth.

🕐 **On the table in 10 minutes** | **Yield: 2 servings as a meal, 4 servings as a side**

1 tbsp (15 ml) avocado oil

2 large cloves garlic, minced

1 tsp minced fresh ginger

3 green onions, sliced thin, whites and greens separated

1 tbsp (8 g) tapioca starch, to thicken (optional)

4 cups (960 ml) chicken broth

1 tbsp (15 ml) coconut aminos

2 tsp (10 ml) toasted sesame oil

4 large eggs, well-beaten

Fine Himalayan salt and freshly cracked black pepper, to taste

Heat a medium pot or saucepan over medium heat until hot. Add the oil and swirl to coat the bottom of the pan. Add the garlic, ginger and white parts of the green onions and sauté until fragrant, about 1 minute.

If using tapioca starch to thicken the soup, take 1 cup (240 ml) of the broth and dissolve the starch in it. Pour the broth, coconut aminos and toasted sesame oil into the pan. Bring the broth to a gentle simmer, and then immediately remove the pot from the heat. Use a spoon to stir the broth continuously in one direction while pouring the eggs into the broth in a thin, steady stream. Using a measuring cup with a spout is helpful for pouring the eggs. This technique will yield soft, creamy egg ribbons in the soup. Season with salt and pepper to taste. Serve immediately, and garnish each bowl with the green onion greens.

Super Green Soup

This soup is a delicious way to work more greens and nutrient-powerhouse cruciferous vegetables into your diet. Ginger, cilantro and lime give this soup a vibrant, memorable flavor, and it is super creamy thanks to the cauliflower. This is sure to become a family favorite, even for the picky eaters!

🕐 **On the table in 20 minutes** | **Yield: 6–8 servings**

2 crowns broccoli (about 1 lb [454 g])

1 small head cauliflower (less than 2 lbs [907 g])

1 tbsp (15 ml) extra-virgin olive oil

1 medium onion, chopped

3–4 celery stalks, thinly sliced

3 carrots, peeled and thinly sliced

2 tsp (12 g) fine Himalayan salt, or more to taste

6 large cloves garlic

1 tbsp (14 g) minced fresh ginger

¼ tsp freshly cracked black pepper, or more to taste

½ tsp dried oregano

4 cups (960 ml) chicken or vegetable broth

6 oz (170 g) baby spinach

½ bunch cilantro, coarsely chopped (about 1 cup [16 g])

2 tbsp (30 ml) fresh lime juice (about 2 limes)

½ cup (120 ml) coconut milk or ½ ripe Hass avocado, to thicken (optional)

¼ cup (35 g) pumpkin seeds

Sliced green onions, to garnish (optional)

Remove the stalks from the broccoli and cauliflower and separate them into florets. Set them aside.

Heat a 5-quart (5-L) or larger pot with a lid over medium heat for 4 to 5 minutes. Add the olive oil and swirl to coat the bottom. Add the onion, celery, carrots and salt and cook for about 5 minutes. Add the garlic and ginger and cook for 1 minute. Add the black pepper, oregano, chicken broth, broccoli and cauliflower florets to the pot and increase the heat to high to bring the mixture to a boil. Cover and reduce the heat to maintain a gentle simmer. Cook for 10 minutes, or until the broccoli and cauliflower florets are just tender. Note that the broth won't completely cover the vegetables.

Remove the pot from the stovetop, add the spinach and cilantro and stir until wilted. Add the lime juice and use an immersion blender to purée the soup, or transfer it to a blender and carefully blend. For a thicker, richer soup, you can add either the coconut milk or avocado and blend again. Taste the soup and add more salt and pepper, if needed. You can either stir the pumpkin seeds into the full batch of soup or serve each bowl with some as a garnish, alongside a garnish of sliced green onions.

Substitutions: You can substitute another leafy green in the place of the spinach. Chard works especially well. Also, if you're running low on broth, you can use plain water.

MAKE IT A MEAL: While the broccoli and cauliflower are simmering, you can cook up some protein to add to the soup. I recommend pan-searing chicken breast according to the instructions on page 22. You could also use the Spicy Italian Sausage (page 52) or simply brown some ground meat seasoned with salt and pepper to mix into the puréed soup.

Fire-Roasted Salsa Soup with Chicken

You could also call this "chicken tortilla-less soup," but I prefer not to focus on what's missing. This soup is bursting with flavor to make your whole family happy for mealtime, and nobody will think it is missing anything. Know what? When I was a kid I did call chicken tortilla soup "salsa soup," because that's what it tastes like. If you really want some crunch in this soup to mimic tortilla strips, you can garnish it with Paleo-friendly plantain chips. Either way you serve it, this is one of my favorite dishes in this book!

On the table in 30 minutes | Yield: 6 servings

1½ tsp (9 g) fine Himalayan salt

1 tsp cumin

½ tsp granulated garlic

½ tsp granulated onion

½ tsp freshly cracked black pepper

4 large boneless, skinless chicken breasts (around 2 lbs [907 g])

1 tbsp (15 ml) avocado oil

Double batch of Shortcut Fire-Roasted Salsa (page 157)

2–4 cups (480–960 ml) chicken bone broth or water

1 onion, chopped

4 cloves garlic, minced

2 tbsp (30 ml) fresh lime juice, or more to taste

1 Hass avocado, thinly sliced, to garnish

½ bunch cilantro, to garnish

1 lime, cut into wedges, to garnish

Sliced jalapeños, to garnish (optional)

Paleo plantain chips (green or ripe, both work), to garnish (optional)

Mix the salt, cumin, garlic, onion and pepper together in a small bowl. Pat the chicken breasts dry and then sprinkle both sides with the seasonings. Heat a 5-quart (5-L) or larger pot with a lid over medium heat until hot. Add the oil and swirl it around to coat the bottom. Sear the breasts for 4 to 5 minutes per side, until they easily release from the pot and are golden brown.

While the chicken is cooking, make the double batch of Shortcut Fire-Roasted Salsa (page 157).

Pour the broth into the pot to deglaze it. Add the salsa, onion, garlic and lime juice and bring the mixture to a low boil over medium-high heat. Cover and reduce the heat to a gentle simmer. Cook for 10 to 12 minutes, or until the chicken is cooked through. Transfer the chicken to a cutting board and either cut it into bite-size pieces or shred it with 2 forks. Return the chicken to the pot and simmer for a few more minutes. Taste and adjust the seasonings as desired. Serve each bowl with a garnish of avocado slices, fresh cilantro, a lime wedge, a slice of fresh jalapeño (if using) and a few plantain chips (if using).

Chef's Note: There are many brands that cook plantain chips in Paleo-friendly fats now, and they can be found at international grocery stores as well as a few mainstream stores. Look for coconut oil, palm oil or avocado oil on the ingredients list.

Irish Lamb Stew

Traditional Irish stew is quite simple, usually only including lamb stewing meat, potatoes, onion and either parsley or thyme. Using ground lamb makes stew possible on a weeknight, and I really enjoy adding in a variety of lower-carb roots, especially rutabaga. Feel free to adjust the ratio of the roots used in this soup to suit your liking. This is an incredible dish to warm your bones on a cold winter's night.

🕐 **On the table in 30 minutes** | **Yield: 4–6 servings**

2 tsp (10 ml) avocado oil

1 lb (454 g) ground lamb

1 large onion, chopped

4 cloves garlic, minced

½ lb (226 g) carrots, peeled and cut into ½" (1-cm) coins (about 3 medium carrots)

½ lb (226 g) parsnips, peeled and cut into ½" (1-cm) coins (about 2 parsnips)

½ lb (226 g) rutabaga, peeled and cubed (about 1 rutabaga)

½ lb (226 g) purple-top turnip, peeled and cubed (about 1 turnip)

¾ lb (340 g) russet potatoes, peeled and cubed (about 2 small potatoes)

1 tbsp (18 g) fine Himalayan salt

1 tsp freshly cracked black pepper

1½ tsp (2 g) dried thyme

4 cups (960 ml) beef bone broth

1 tsp apple cider vinegar

Heat a 5-quart (5-L) or larger pot with a lid for several minutes over medium heat until hot. Swirl the oil to coat the bottom. Brown the lamb for about 5 minutes. You may wish to strain off some of the rendered fat at this point for a lighter soup.

Add the onion and garlic and cook for 2 minutes. Add the carrots, parsnips, rutabaga, turnip, potatoes, salt, pepper, thyme and broth and bring to a low boil. Cover, reduce the heat to maintain a simmer and cook for 15 to 20 minutes, or until everything is fork tender. Stir in the vinegar at the end and taste, adjusting the seasonings as needed.

Zuppa Toscana

Zuppa Toscana is a rich, creamy sausage and kale soup that's bursting with flavor and is so comforting, especially on a chilly evening. The potatoes and bacon make this a dish that really sticks to your ribs and leaves you feeling oh-so-satisfied after enjoying a bowl (or two).

 On the table in 40 minutes | **Yield: 4-6 servings**

½ lb (226 g) bacon, cut into 1" (2.5-cm) pieces

1 medium onion, chopped

1 lb (454 g) Spicy Italian Sausage (page 52) or store-bought

4 cups (960 ml) chicken bone broth

1 lb (454 g) russet potatoes, peeled and cubed (about 3 potatoes)

4 large cloves garlic, minced

½ tsp red pepper flakes

½ tsp fine Himalayan salt

¼ tsp freshly cracked black pepper

3–4 cups (192–259 g) roughly chopped kale, stems removed

1–2 tsp (5–10 ml) apple cider vinegar, to taste

¾–1 cup (180–240 ml) canned full-fat coconut milk (optional)

Add the bacon to a 5-quart (5-L) or larger pot and heat it over medium heat to crisp the bacon, about 10 to 15 minutes, depending on the thickness of the bacon. Set it aside.

Cook the onion in the bacon fat for 2 to 3 minutes, and then crumble in the sausage and cook for about 7 minutes, until the sausage is mostly cooked through. Pour in the chicken broth and scrape the bottom of the pan. Add the potatoes, garlic, red pepper flakes, salt and pepper.

Raise the heat to high to bring the soup to a low boil, and then cover and lower the heat to a simmer. Cook until the potatoes are fork tender, about 15 to 20 minutes. Stir in the kale to wilt it and add the vinegar. Stir in the coconut milk, if using. Taste and add salt and pepper to taste, and then serve with the crisp bacon as a garnish on top.

*See photo on page 124.

Brisk Borscht

Using ground beef instead of stew meat and a food processor to shred all of the vegetables reduces the prep and cooking time significantly for this vibrant soup. Plus, ground beef is typically much more budget friendly and is the most affordable cut of grass-fed beef. Even people who say they don't like beets will enjoy this tangy, rich and subtly sweet soup.

🕐 **On the table in 40 minutes** | **Yield: 6 servings**

1½ lbs (680 g) ground beef

2½ tsp (15 g) fine Himalayan salt

¼ tsp freshly cracked black pepper

2 lbs (907 g) beets, peeled, greens reserved for Spiced Beet Greens (page 104)

1 medium yellow or white onion, peeled

2 large carrots, peeled

2 cups (140 g) shredded cabbage

6 small cloves garlic, minced

6–7 tbsp (90–105 ml) fresh lemon juice (about 3 lemons)

2 cups (480 ml) beef broth

1 (½-oz [14-g]) package fresh dill, minced, one sprig reserved for garnish

Unsweetened Paleo yogurt or sour cream, for serving (optional)

Heat a 5-quart (5-L) or larger pot with a lid over medium heat until hot. Add the ground beef and sprinkle it with the salt and pepper. Brown for about 8 to 10 minutes, stirring occasionally while you prepare the vegetables.

Use a food processor with a disc attachment (large holes) to shred the beets, onion, carrots and cabbage. Add the vegetables and the garlic to the pot with the beef. It's okay if the beef hasn't browned completely. Pour in the lemon juice, beef broth and 2 cups (480 ml) water and stir in the dill. Bring the soup to a boil, cover, reduce the heat to a gentle simmer and cook for 15 to 20 minutes.

Taste and adjust the salt, if needed. If you like, serve each bowl with a dollop of unsweetened Paleo-friendly yogurt or sour cream alternative on top. Take the optionally reserved sprig of fresh dill, mince it and sprinkle it on top as a garnish.

Chef's Notes: There are a number of brands of nut-based, Paleo-friendly yogurts and sour creams available at many grocery stores. Just make sure to read the ingredient labels.

Use the leftover partial head of cabbage to make a few Cabbage Steaks (page 37) to pair with another main dish.

If you are out of beef broth, just use all water for this soup.

DESSERTS

None of the desserts in this chapter require any Paleo flours. Because, really . . . who has time to fool around with finicky baked goods after a long day at work and after cooking a full meal? These are all simple, yet delicious (some dangerously so!) sweet treats that can be whipped up quickly right before you'd like to eat them, or in a few cases, take mere minutes to prepare but do need additional time to chill before you can enjoy them.

← See recipe on page 144.

Rich Dark Chocolate Chia Pudding

Chia seed pudding takes mere moments to prepare, but you do have to wait several hours for it to set in the refrigerator before you can enjoy it. You can either do it in the morning before you leave for work so that you can enjoy it that evening, or prepare it one night for enjoyment the next day. For a portable snack, add the ingredients directly to a jar with a lid so you can grab it and go. Chia seeds are a great source of fiber and plant-based omega-3 fatty acids, making this a nutritious treat.

🕐 **On the table in 5 minutes (sort of)** | **Yield: 2 servings**

3 tbsp (30 g) chia seeds

2 tbsp (11 g) cocoa powder

Pinch of fine Himalayan salt

¾ cup (180 ml) canned full-fat coconut milk

¼ cup (60 ml) water

1 tbsp (15 ml) maple syrup

¼ tsp vanilla extract

Optional toppings and add ins: chopped nuts, seeds, a swirl of nut or seed butter, chopped fresh fruit and/or shredded unsweetened coconut

Add the chia seeds, cocoa powder and salt to a glass container with a lid and stir everything together with a small whisk or fork. Add the coconut milk, water, maple syrup and vanilla and stir again to remove any clumps. The consistency will be thin, but due to the high content of soluble fiber in chia seeds, they will swell in size as they sit in the coconut milk, creating what is known as chia seed "gel," which is responsible for the thick, creamy consistency after several hours.

You can put it in the refrigerator immediately, but you can also let it sit for about 10 minutes and stir one more time before chilling. This second stir can help prevent any clumps of chia from forming. Refrigerate it for at least 4 hours before serving. Enjoy as is or include some optional toppings or add ins. There is a lot of room for experimentation with chia seed pudding!

Chef's Note: You can use your favorite dairy-free milk alternative like almond milk, cashew milk, tigernut milk, etc. in place of coconut milk or water, but if you are not making your own, be sure to read the labels and watch for additives, thickeners and sweeteners.

Mango-Lime Avocado Mousse

This avocado mousse is a dish that tastes like dessert but is truly a nutritious snack or small meal replacement full of healthy fats and protein. Puddings and mousses made from avocados are nothing new, but I have found that combining avocado with another fruit yields a much more desirable texture than avocado alone. Plus it opens up the possibilities for so many flavor combinations. Mango and lime is just one option!

🕐 **On the table in less than 15 minutes** | **Yield: 2 servings**

2 yellow mangoes (about 1 lb [454 g])

1 Hass avocado (about ½ lb [226 g])

¼ cup (60 ml) fresh lime juice (about 2 limes)

Pinch of fine Himalayan salt

3 tbsp (27 g) hydrolyzed collagen (see page 168 for more info)

1 tbsp (15 ml) honey, or to taste (optional)

¼–⅓ cup (23–31 g) finely shredded unsweetened coconut

Use a sharp paring knife to peel the mangoes and cut away the fruit from the hard center core. Add the fruit to a food processor with an S-blade attachment. Peel the avocado and discard the seed. Coarsely chop the avocado and add it to the food processor with the mango. Squeeze in the lime juice. Add the salt and collagen.

Pulse the food processor until the ingredients have combined to form a smooth, thick mousse. Scrape down the sides with a spatula once or twice while processing. Taste to see if you'd like to add any honey for added sweetness. Transfer the mousse to a glass bowl with a lid and stir in the shredded coconut. You can eat it immediately or allow it to chill in the refrigerator.

Chef's Notes: You can take this base recipe of 1 part avocado to approximately 2 parts fruit and experiment with other flavors using what is in season. I also really enjoy cherry-vanilla and blueberry–cocoa powder.

If you don't have hydrolyzed collagen, you can omit it, but I recommend using it since it adds valuable amino acids and protein to the dish.

Carrot Cake Date Energy Balls

Energy balls are a sort of snack-dessert hybrid. They're full of healthy fats and protein from the pecans and coconut, are sweetened only with dates, and even sneak in some vegetables with the carrots. This blend really does taste like carrot cake bites and is kid approved.

🕐 **On the table in 15 minutes** | **Yield: 20–24 balls**

8 oz (226 g) carrots, peeled

1 cup (110 g) pecans

1 cup (93 g) finely shredded unsweetened coconut, plus extra for garnish

1 tsp cinnamon

¼ tsp fine Himalayan salt, or more to taste

10 pitted Medjool dates

½ tsp vanilla extract

Add the carrots, pecans, coconut, cinnamon, salt, dates and vanilla to the bowl of a food processor with the S-blade attached. Pulse until everything is finely crumbled. Taste and add more salt, if needed.

Use a measuring spoon to get about 2 tablespoons (30 g) of the mixture and roll it between your palms to make a ball. If you want, roll the balls in a little extra shredded coconut for visual appeal. These can be eaten right away or chilled in the refrigerator. Store in the refrigerator for up to 5 days.

Baked Spiced Pears with Honey

This is a recipe that my acupuncturist instructed me to eat one year during the fall and winter. I had caught a really bad case of bronchitis, and he told me that in traditional Chinese medicine this dish is used to help support the lungs. Also according to TCM, the kidneys need extra TLC during the winter, and walnuts give that support, taste delicious and add a great texture to the pears. This dish is so incredibly easy and comforting, and now I look forward to it on cool, cozy fall and winter nights.

On the table in 30 minutes | **Yield: 2–4 servings**

2 Asian pears (or any other variety), cut in half and cored

2 tsp (10 ml) melted coconut oil

About ¼ tsp ground cinnamon

About ⅛ tsp ginger powder

Few small pinches of fine Himalayan salt

¼ cup (29 g) chopped walnuts (or other nut)

2–4 tbsp (30–60 ml) raw honey, for serving

Preheat the oven to 350°F (180°C).

If the cut and cored pears don't lay flat with the cut side up, slice a sliver off the back so that they will. Rub the coconut oil over each pear half. Sprinkle the cinnamon, ginger and salt on top and add the walnuts to the hole created from removing the core. Arrange the pears in a single layer on a metal baking sheet and bake for about 20 to 25 minutes, or until tender. Drizzle with the honey before serving.

Chef's Note: If you don't own a melon baller, just use a spoon to core the pears after cutting them in half.

Flourless Chocolate Chip Cookies

As a kid I remember being mystified by flourless peanut butter cookies. It was so curious to me that they would hold together and had a crumb just like normal cookies. This is a Paleo version of that classic recipe my mom would make for me, swapping in almond butter for the peanut butter (peanuts are a legume, not a nut) and using better-for-you unrefined coconut sugar. Be careful with these: They are dangerously delicious!

🕐 **On the table in 30 minutes** | **Yield: approximately 14 cookies**

1 cup (258 g) creamy almond butter

¾ cup (150 g) coconut sugar

1 large egg

½ cup (84 g) dark chocolate chips

1 tsp vanilla extract

½ tsp baking soda

⅛ tsp fine Himalayan salt

Flaked sea salt, to sprinkle on top

Preheat the oven to 350°F (180°C) and line a metal baking sheet with parchment paper.

In a bowl, mix together the almond butter, coconut sugar, egg, chocolate chips, vanilla, baking soda and salt to form a thick, uniform batter. Use a tablespoon to scoop up a heaping amount of batter and place it on the lined baking sheet, leaving about 2 inches (5 cm) of space between the cookies. Use the tines of a fork to flatten each cookie, and then rotate the tines 90 degrees and press again to make a crisscross pattern on the top of the cookie.

Bake the cookies for about 10 to 12 minutes, until they have darkened but the edges aren't yet browned. Cool the cookies directly on the pan, allowing them to cool completely before serving, as they are very fragile while warm. Sprinkle with the flaked salt before serving.

Chef's Note: Coconut sugar can make it hard to judge when baked goods have finished cooking, since it makes the dough quite dark when raw. Some will argue that organic cane sugar isn't Paleo, but if you prefer a lighter cookie you can use that. Do not use a liquid sweetener like honey or maple syrup, as the recipe depends on the granulated sugar for the crumb.

Salted Chocolate Chip Cookie Dough Freezer Fudge

I did the happy dance when I tasted this recipe. The magic of tahini, maple syrup and vanilla come together to truly taste just like raw cookie dough. You can eat this less than an hour after preparing it, but these bites of freezer fudge reach their ideal consistency after being frozen overnight if you can stand to wait that long to dive in.

On the table in 45 minutes to 1 hour | **Yield: 10 servings**

1 cup (258 g) tahini

⅓ cup (80 ml) melted coconut oil

⅓ cup (80 ml) dark robust maple syrup

2 tsp (10 ml) vanilla extract

¼ tsp fine Himalayan salt

¼ cup (42 g) plus 2 tbsp (21 g) dark chocolate chips, divided

Flaked sea salt, to sprinkle on top

Line a freezer-safe glass container or loaf pan with parchment paper. (An 8 x 8–inch [20 x 20–cm] baking dish works well.) In a medium bowl, mix together the tahini, coconut oil, maple syrup, vanilla and salt. Stir until it all comes together evenly; it may take a minute or so. Stir in the ¼ cup (42 g) of chocolate chips, pour the mixture into the lined dish and place it in the freezer. After about 20 to 30 minutes, sprinkle the remaining chocolate chips on top.

After about 45 minutes, the fudge will be firm enough to eat, but if you can wait at least 60 minutes that is more ideal. It will be even firmer after it's been frozen overnight. Use a butter knife to cut it into squares and discard the parchment paper. Sprinkle with the flaked sea salt. Serve it immediately or return it to the freezer as it does start to melt if kept at room temperature. Store it in the freezer for up to 3 months in a covered container.

Chef's Note: On the night you want to eat this, make dessert first before starting to cook dinner. It will firm up and freeze while you are cooking and eating your meal. Also, if you want to mix things up, replace the chocolate chips with chopped nuts such as pecans or walnuts, or do a mix of chocolate chips and nuts.

SAUCES

Sauces can elevate a boring meal into something extraordinary. I always have at least 2 homemade sauces in my refrigerator at all times to jazz up everything from sautéed greens to steak. You'll also find one very special non-sauce recipe in this chapter, too: version 2.0 of my famous "tapioca cheese," which I'm calling Fresh Mozzarella here. It doesn't matter what you're cooking; if you pair it with one of the recipes from this chapter, it will be exciting and delicious.

← See recipe on page 155.

Comeback Sauce

Comeback sauce is a classic Deep South condiment that gets its name for being so good it'll make you come back for more. Many regions and other countries have their own versions of a mayonnaise-and-ketchup-based spicy sauce like this. It's kind of a lazy version of a remoulade that works as a replacement for it. Serve it with seafood (especially the Kickin' Salmon Patties on page 79), on burgers or dip your fries in it.

🕐 **On the table in less than 5 minutes** | **Yield: approximately ³/₄ cup (180 ml)**

½ cup (120 ml) mayonnaise

¼ cup (60 ml) ketchup

2 tbsp (30 ml) fresh lemon juice

1–2 tsp (5–10 ml) Louisiana-style hot sauce (omit for a mild sauce)

1 tsp fine Himalayan salt

1 tsp granulated garlic

1 tsp granulated onion

1 tsp freshly cracked black pepper

½ tsp smoked paprika

¼ tsp cayenne pepper

Combine the mayonnaise, ketchup, lemon juice, hot sauce, salt, garlic, onion, pepper, paprika and cayenne in a glass container with a lid and stir until a uniform sauce forms. Serve alongside the Kickin' Salmon Patties on page 79, the Crispy Baked Rosemary Garlic Steak Fries on page 120 or with the Crispy Roasted Brussels Sprouts on page 115.

Keeps in the refrigerator for about 1 week.

2-Minute Marinara

This definitely is not an authentic, made from-scratch marinara sauce, but it sure is easy and surprisingly delicious. While canned foods shouldn't make up the bulk of our diets, it's okay to use them sometimes to save time and sanity. After all, humans have been using various preservation methods to keep food fresh for millennia. This sauce may look deceptively simple, but I promise it is flavor-packed and the perfect thing for topping a meatza (page 65) or the Easy No-Breading Chicken Parmesan (page 30). It's also amazing to dip steak fries (page 120) in. I'm sure you'll come up with other uses for it, too.

🕐 **On the table in less than 5 minutes** │ **Yield: 1 cup (240 ml)**

1 (8-oz [226-g]) can plain tomato sauce

½ tsp fine Himalayan salt, or to taste

½ tsp dried oregano

½ tsp dried basil

¼ tsp granulated garlic

¼ tsp granulated onion

¼ tsp freshly cracked black pepper

In a medium bowl, mix together the tomato sauce, salt, oregano, basil, garlic, onion and pepper, stirring to make sure none of the spices clump together.

This will keep in the refrigerator for 5 to 7 days.

Carolina Mustard BBQ Sauce

Different regions have their own distinctive ways of making BBQ sauce, and South Carolina is known for mustard sauces like this. It is a great alternative to a tomato-based sauce and can function as a flavorful honey mustard sauce, too.

 On the table in less than 5 minutes | **Yield: approximately ³/₄ cup (180 ml)**

½ cup (120 ml) prepared yellow mustard

¼ cup (60 ml) plus 2 tbsp (30 ml) apple cider vinegar

1 tbsp (15 ml) raw honey

2 tsp (10 ml) coconut aminos

1 tsp fine Himalayan salt

1 tsp granulated onion

1 tsp granulated garlic

½ tsp freshly cracked black pepper

½ tsp dried rosemary

½ tsp dried thyme

¼ tsp celery seed

¼–½ tsp cayenne pepper (optional)

In a medium bowl, mix together the mustard, vinegar, honey, coconut aminos, salt, onion, garlic, pepper, rosemary, thyme, celery seed and cayenne (if using). Stir to combine.

This keeps in the refrigerator for about a week.

Avocado Crema

This sauce is the perfect combination of thick, creamy and cheesy to make you forget that you're eating something totally free of dairy. It's a refreshingly cool sauce that's great to pair with spicier fare.

 On the table in less than 5 minutes | **Yield: approximately ¾ cup (180 ml)**

1 Hass avocado, peeled and seed removed

2 tbsp (30 ml) fresh lime juice (about 2 limes)

3 large cloves garlic, peeled

¼ cup (60 ml) canned full-fat coconut milk

½ tbsp (4 g) nutritional yeast

¾ tsp fine Himalayan salt, or more to taste

Add the avocado, lime juice, garlic, coconut milk, nutritional yeast and salt to the bowl of a food processor with an S-blade or to a blender and blitz until smooth. Serve with the Crispy Brazilian Chicken Wings (page 42) or any other meat dish (like a steak, pork chop or fillet of fish) that needs a sauce to liven it up.

This is best if used within 24 hours, but it will keep in the fridge for 3 to 4 days.

Shortcut Fire-Roasted Salsa

Even as an extremely picky child, I always loved salsa. I would say I am a bit of a salsa connoisseur and look forward every year to summer, when I can make the freshest of fresh salsas from my garden tomatoes and jalapeños. But what about the rest of the year? Canned fire-roasted tomatoes are where it's at for the best flavor and texture outside of peak summer. Don't let the simplicity of this recipe fool you. It is so flavorful!

🕐 **On the table in 5 minutes** | **Yield: approximately 2¹/₂ cups (600 ml)**

1–2 jalapeño or serrano peppers, coarsely chopped

1 (15-oz [426-g]) can fire-roasted tomatoes

1 tbsp (15 ml) fresh lime juice (about 1 lime)

1–1½ tsp (6–9 g) fine Himalayan salt

½ medium white onion, coarsely chopped

2 cloves garlic, peeled

1 packed cup (20 g) fresh cilantro, thick lower stems removed

Add the peppers, tomatoes, lime juice, salt, onion, garlic and cilantro to the bowl of a food processor with the S-blade attachment. Pulse until the desired smooth texture is achieved. Taste and adjust seasonings as desired.

Use this to make Huevos Ahogados with Plantain Tortillas (page 26) or make a double recipe to use as the base of the Fire-Roasted Salsa Soup with Chicken (page 131).

This is best if eaten within 2 days, but it will keep in the refrigerator for 5 to 7 days.

Chef's Notes: If you prefer to use fresh tomatoes while they are in season, simply replace the canned tomatoes with 1 lb (454 g) of fresh tomatoes. San Marzano and Roma tomatoes are excellent choices.

Also, when cutting the hot peppers, note that it is not the seeds that are hot (this is a widely perpetuated myth among food blogs/cookbooks); instead, it is the pith (AKA ribs) that have the highest concentration of capsaicin. This is the white, spongy flesh running vertically along the inner wall of the fruit and includes the part of the pepper that the seeds are attached to near where the stem attaches. So, if you want to significantly reduce the heat of the peppers, scrape the white parts away with a spoon, but don't fret over discarding the seeds.

White BBQ Sauce

If you're not from the Deep South, you may have never heard of white BBQ sauce, which originated in southern Alabama in the early 1900s. It's a creamy, tangy, mayonnaise-based sauce that goes well with so many things, especially chicken, roasted green vegetables and fries.

 On the table in less than 5 minutes | Yield: approximately 1½ cups (360 ml)

1 cup (240 ml) mayonnaise

2 tbsp (30 g) prepared horseradish

⅓ cup (80 ml) apple cider vinegar

1½ tbsp (23 ml) stone ground mustard

2 tsp (4 g) freshly cracked black pepper

2 tsp (12 g) fine Himalayan salt

2 tsp (4 g) granulated garlic

1 tsp paprika (optional)

In a medium bowl, mix together the mayonnaise, horseradish, vinegar, mustard, pepper, salt, garlic and paprika (if using). One batch is enough for cooking 8 chicken thighs according to the recipe for Baked BBQ Chicken Thighs on page 38 with a little leftover to drizzle on top of Crispy Roasted Brussels Sprouts (page 115).

This keeps in the refrigerator for about 1 week.

Memphis BBQ Sauce

I am so proud of this recipe. I have loved Memphis BBQ since I first visited the city as a teenager in the '90s after my sister moved here. Memphis sauce is tomato-and-vinegar-based, tangy, thin and just a little sweet. It is my ideal BBQ sauce, and this version tastes amazingly authentic. There are many suggestions throughout the book for how to use the sauce, but it pretty much goes well with anything. Hope you enjoy it as much as I do!

🕐 **On the table in less than 10 minutes** | **Yield: approximately 2 ³/₄ cups (660 ml)**

4 pitted Medjool dates

¼ cup (60 ml) hot water

1 (7-oz [198-g]) can tomato paste

¼ cup (60 ml) apple cider vinegar

¼ cup (60 ml) prepared yellow mustard

2 tbsp (30 ml) molasses

1 tbsp (15 ml) coconut aminos

2 tsp (4 g) granulated garlic

1 tsp granulated onion

1 tsp fine Himalayan salt

½ tsp celery seed

½ tsp smoked paprika

½ tsp cayenne pepper

Submerge the dates in the hot water and soak for at least 5 minutes. Add the soaked dates and the tomato paste to the bowl of a food processor with the S-blade attachment. Fill the empty tomato paste can with water and add it to the bowl. Repeat to add a total of 14 ounces (414 ml) of water. Add the vinegar, mustard, molasses, coconut aminos, garlic, onion, salt, celery seed, paprika and cayenne. Purée to form a smooth sauce.

This keeps for about 1 week in the refrigerator.

Fresh Mozzarella

This is version 2.0 of my famous Queso Blanco, AKA tapioca cheese that made huge waves in the Paleo and AIP communities with the release of my first book, *Latin American Paleo Cooking*. The original recipe has since been shared publicly on my website and has become a reader favorite. It's hard to top perfection, but I did make a few tweaks to make this meltable, stretchy Paleo cheese even better than the original. You can enjoy it plain or with mixed herbs. I know that for some, giving up dairy is the most difficult part of Paleo, so I hope this enriches your journey and makes it easier.

🕐 **On the table in 10 minutes** | **Yield: approximately 6 oz (170 g)**

FOR THE FRESH MOZZARELLA

½ cup (120 ml) canned full-fat coconut milk

½ tsp salt

1–2 tbsp (8–16 g) nutritional yeast

1 tbsp (15 ml) freshly-squeezed lemon juice

1 clove garlic, minced

¼ tsp granulated garlic

¼ tsp granulated onion

2 tbsp (17 g) tapioca starch dissolved in 2 tbsp (30 ml) water

2 tsp (6 g) gelatin

FOR THE HERBED FRESH MOZZARELLA

To the original recipe add the following:

½ tsp dried basil

½ tsp dried oregano

¼ tsp freshly cracked black pepper

In a small saucepan, whisk together the coconut milk, salt, nutritional yeast, lemon juice, garlic, granulated garlic and onion. (If making the Herbed Fresh Mozzarella, add the basil, oregano and pepper.)

Pour the tapioca slurry into the saucepan and then sprinkle the gelatin on top in a single layer to allow it to bloom. Heat over medium heat, whisking often. It will thicken slowly at first, then after about 6 minutes, it will get much thicker. Keep cooking and whisking constantly until it starts to really stick to itself inside the whisk and you can lift it up from the bottom of the pan. You should see it bubbling at the bottom of the pan. Do not make the mistake of undercooking the cheese. It should be done after about 8 or 9 minutes total, and it will look like a pot of melted cheese when it is done.

You can use it immediately in any of the recipes that call for it: Mozzarella Meatza (page 65), BBQ Chicken Pizza with Plantain Crust (page 33) or Easy No-Breading Chicken Parmesan (page 30). Or you can transfer the contents to a small glass storage container and allow it to set in the fridge over the course of a few hours or overnight. It freezes well, so I recommend doubling or tripling the recipe and keeping some stashed in your freezer to help make meals come together more quickly.

This is best used within 2 to 3 days. Freeze up to 3 months in an airtight container. Defrost in the refrigerator overnight when you are ready to use it.

Beet Marinara

This is an adaptation from one of the most popular recipes on my website. Many years ago, I did an elimination trial for all nightshades (which include tomatoes, peppers, eggplant and potatoes, among others). During that time, I developed the best version of a tomato-less marinara sauce I had ever tasted. This sauce improves on the original by being faster, easier and more flavorful. It's a wonderful way to enjoy beets, even if you do include tomatoes in your diet.

On the table in 30 minutes | **Yield: approximately 4 1/2 cups (1.1 L)**

2 tbsp (30 ml) extra-virgin olive oil

1 onion, chopped

2 ribs celery, chopped

½ lb (226 g) carrots, peeled and thinly sliced

5 cloves garlic, minced

2 medium beets, peeled and thinly chopped

2 cups (480 ml) chicken bone broth (or water)

¼ cup (60 ml) fresh lemon juice (about 2 lemons)

1½ tsp (2 g) dried basil

1 tsp dried oregano

1 tsp dried thyme

2 tsp (12 g) fine Himalayan salt

1 tsp freshly cracked black pepper

8 pitted Kalamata olives (optional)

Heat a 5-quart (5-L) or larger pot with a lid over medium heat for 5 minutes. Add the olive oil and swirl to coat the bottom. Sauté the onion, celery and carrots (AKA mirepoix) together for about 5 to 7 minutes to soften. Add the garlic and beets and cook for a few minutes. Deglaze the pot with the broth. Add the lemon juice, basil, oregano, thyme, salt and pepper and bring to a boil over high heat, cover and reduce heat to a low boil. Cook for 15 minutes, or until the beets are fork tender. Remove from the heat and add the olives if you want some extra umami in the sauce—I highly recommend them.

Purée with a stick blender, or carefully transfer to a blender or food processor to blitz, making sure to allow the steam to vent to avoid an explosion.

This sauce can be served on top of your favorite Paleo vegetable noodles, used to make the Easy No-Breading Chicken Parmesan (page 30) nightshade-free or used as the base for Beet Bolognese with Spaghetti Squash Noodles (page 73).

This keeps in the refrigerator for 3 to 5 days, or in the freezer for up to 3 months.

Caulifredo Sauce

If you've never made a caulifredo sauce before, you are sure in for a treat. When you taste this decadently rich and creamy Alfredo sauce, you won't believe it is made out of cauliflower and without any heavy cream! Puréed cauliflower is an incredible thickener thanks to the pectin in it. It doesn't even need any coconut milk to help it out. This sauce can really be eaten by itself as a soup, but I highly recommend making Chicken Caulifredo with Steamed Broccoli (page 22) with it. This makes a big batch, and I did this intentionally so that you don't have to use only a partial head of cauliflower and wonder what to do with the rest of it. Trust me: You'll be glad you have so much sauce!

On the table in 30 minutes | **Yield: approximately 5 cups (1.2 L)**

1 tbsp (15 ml) extra-virgin olive oil

1 white onion, chopped

6 large cloves garlic, minced

1 large head cauliflower (about 2¼ lbs [1 kg]), florets only

2 cups (480 ml) chicken broth (or water)

¼ cup (32 g) nutritional yeast

1 tbsp (15 ml) fresh lemon juice

2½ tsp (15 g) fine Himalayan salt

½ tsp freshly cracked black pepper

Heat a 5-quart (5-L) or larger pot with a lid over medium heat until hot. Add the oil and swirl to coat the bottom. Add the onion and cook for 5 minutes. Add the garlic and cook until fragrant, about 1 minute. Add the cauliflower florets, chicken broth, nutritional yeast, lemon juice, salt and pepper and bring to a low boil over medium-high heat. Cover and reduce the heat to a simmer and cook until the cauliflower is fork tender, about 7 to 9 minutes.

Use an immersion blender to blend the sauce, or for a smoother purée, transfer the contents carefully to a food processor or blender and blitz until smooth, being careful to vent the steam according to your machine's directions. Serve as part of Chicken Caulifredo with Steamed Broccoli (page 22).

This keeps in the refrigerator for 4 to 5 days, or in the freezer for up to 3 months.

> **Chef's Note:** If you are using pre-cut cauliflower florets, you need about 1½ lbs (680 g) for this recipe.

Tools You'll Need

There are a couple of kitchen tools you will need in addition to your oven to make all of the recipes in this book. Remember, you can scan the QR code on page 11 to be taken to an updated page on my website that will link to specific brands I use in my own kitchen.

FOOD PROCESSOR, WITH S-BLADE AND LARGE SHREDDING DISC

This makes quick work of prepping vegetables and creates smooth, creamy sauces.

ZESTER

Using the zest of citrus is an incredible way to add a punch of flavor to your cooking.

IMMERSION BLENDER

This allows you to purée soups and cooked sauces right in the pot in which you cooked them. It's so much easier than transferring piping hot food to a blender!

SHARP KNIFE

This may be obvious, but I can't emphasize enough how important owning one good, very sharp knife is. I like to use a Santoku knife for all my chopping, slicing and dicing needs and almost never need to pull a different knife out.

MEAT THERMOMETER

Test, don't guess! Due to variations in cookware, stovetops, sizes of cuts of meat, etc., the only surefire way to know when your meat is done is to use a thermometer and check the temperature.

GARLIC PRESS

A high-quality garlic press that you can use without peeling the garlic first can save so much time, preventing the need to manually mince the garlic. I remember balking at the idea of spending $40 on a really high quality one back in 2010, but I think mine will last a lifetime, and I am thankful for it every day.

Stocking Your Paleo Pantry

When writing this book, I wanted to keep the specialty ingredients to a minimum and focus on fresh meats, vegetables and herbs. But there are a couple of pantry items that are worth keeping on hand to really elevate your Paleo cooking. All of these items should be easily available at your local grocery stores, but if not, you can order them online from a number of retailers.

For links to specific brands that I use, scan the QR code on page 11 to be taken to a resources page for this cookbook on my website.

BONE BROTH

You can make and freeze your own bone broth. (See my first book, *Latin American Paleo Cooking*, or my website, www.thecuriouscoconut.com, for instructions.) Or you can purchase pre-made broth. There are several options now that come frozen or in shelf-stable Tetra Paks. I always keep a carton or two in my pantry for emergencies and try to also keep a few quarts of homemade in my freezer, but sometimes I lapse. For this book, using bone broth that comes in cartons is great, because it stays fresh in the fridge for about 10 days. Look for brands that just use bones, vegetables and seasonings.

COCONUT AMINOS

This is a gluten-free and legume-free alternative to soy sauce made from the nectar of coconut blossoms. The flavor is not as intense as soy sauce and it has a hint of sweetness. It is now widely available, even at mainstream grocery stores. Look for it either near the soy sauce, or sometimes, confusingly, near the peanut butter.

HYDROLYZED COLLAGEN AND GELATIN

Collagen is the primary protein found in our connective tissue, skin and bones, and gelatin is extracted from collagen that has been cooked long enough for the amino acids to begin breaking down. That is why bone broth is a good source of gelatin.

Hydrolyzed collagen is the type of collagen you'll see sold as a supplement, which just means it has been broken down further in a nontoxic process that involves water (hence "hydro-"). Both gelatin and hydrolyzed collagen have some impressive scientific evidence backing them up as healthful additions to our diets, especially for our hair, skin, joint and nail health. They may also aid sleep and digestion. This is thanks to the unique makeup of amino acids that help complement and balance out the amino acids found in meats. The notable amino acids found in both gelatin and collagen are glycine, proline, glutamic acid and lysine.

Culinarily speaking, here's what you need to know about the two:

Gelatin is only soluble in hot liquids, and it must be "bloomed" first by sprinkling it on top of a small amount of room-temperature water to hydrate and plump it up. Then, it must be dissolved in hot liquid. Once it cools, it will set the liquid (think: Jell-O®). It can also be used to help make sauces thicker, as you'll see in this book.

Hydrolyzed collagen, on the other hand, has no gelling powers, and it can be fully dissolved in room-temperature or even cool liquids. This makes it easy to take as a supplement by adding it to water and simply drinking it. It can also help add some body and smoothness to sauces and other recipes. You'll see it in this book added to a few dishes to enhance both the texture and nutrition.

I prefer to use hydrolyzed collagen and gelatin that have been sourced from pasture-raised, grass-fed cows. There are several options available on the market, some of which are no more expensive than the kind derived from conventionally-raised animals.

NUTRITIONAL YEAST

Nutritional yeast is used to give the recipes in this book a delicious savory, cheesy flavor. It also happens to be packed with many vitamins (especially niacin, B5 and B6), minerals and fiber. Look for a brand that does not use synthetic vitamins to fortify the yeast. The ingredients should only state "dried yeast" or "Saccharomyces cerevisiae," which is the species of yeast used to make it. Nutritional yeast is not the same thing as brewer's yeast and is naturally gluten-free.

TAPIOCA STARCH

I tried to avoid using any flours in this book, but there are a couple of instances where you do need to use a little starch, and my famous meltable cheese depends on starch for its magical stretching properties. This is another common, inexpensive ingredient available at mainstream grocery stores or smaller international markets. Tapioca is the starch that has been extracted from the yuca (cassava) root. Note that it is not the same thing as cassava flour, which is the whole root ground and dried, and they cannot be used interchangeably.

TOASTED SESAME OIL

Toasted sesame oil gives so much flavor to food and is a common, inexpensive ingredient at both mainstream grocery stores and smaller Asian markets. Sometimes the bottles don't state "toasted;" however, if you look at the oil and it is a rich, dark brown color, that means it is toasted. Fresh sesame oil has a very light color, almost blonde, and I've never actually seen it available in a grocery store.

UNREFINED SALT

I prefer to use a finely ground Himalayan pink salt, but you can also use an unrefined sea salt. Unrefined salts contain important trace minerals to help balance out the sodium.

Sourcing Meats, Vegetables and Fats

MEATS

The Paleo diet encourages us to source the best-raised meats we can. This means for beef and lamb to seek out grass-fed and grass-finished if it is available and can fit your budget. Pasture-raised but grain-finished is the next best option. For chicken, look for pasture-raised birds; free range is not the same thing. Pork is also ideally pasture-raised. The tides are changing in the farming industry, and you are now able to find grass-fed and pasture-raised meats at large national retailers like Target and Aldi. You may also have local farmers who sell at farmers markets or in bulk. It can be well worth the investment in a chest freezer to be able to buy a quarter of a grass-fed cow or half a pig in bulk for a very low price per pound to feed you for months.

If you are unable to source these kinds of meats locally, there are numerous options for ordering online. If they do not fit into your budget, please don't feel ashamed and just do the best that you can do. I personally think that it is better to invest in well-raised meats and buy conventional (non-organic) produce to save money.

VEGETABLES

I am a big fan of the Environmental Working Group for the work they do each year on the "Clean Fifteen and Dirty Dozen" list for produce, which ranks pesticide contamination of 47 of the most popular fruits and vegetables. The least contaminated are the "Clean Fifteen" and the most contaminated are the "Dirty Dozen." A great way to save money on your produce budget is to opt for conventional (rather than organic) for all of the Clean Fifteen items. I do my best to always either buy organic or locally grown Dirty Dozen items (or grow them myself in my garden).

AVOCADO OIL

Avocado oil is used in this book for high-heat applications as it has the highest smoke point of any Paleo oil, up to 500°F (260°C). Make sure to get refined, not virgin, avocado oil, and choose a brand that expeller-presses the oil, uses a natural refining process (not solvent-based with hexane) and is unbleached. Virgin avocado oil has a much lower smoke point of around 350 to 375°F (180 to 190°C).

COCONUT OIL

Coconut oil is great to use in desserts because it enhances the sweetness of whatever you cook with it. For that same reason it's also fantastic to use for roasting sweet potatoes or frying ripe plantains. Opt for unrefined, expeller-pressed coconut oil, which will have a light coconutty flavor. For minimal coconut flavor, get a naturally refined version meeting the same standards as described for avocado oil.

EXTRA-VIRGIN OLIVE OIL

Somehow a myth got started in the Paleo community that extra-virgin olive oil is dangerous to cook with and that it should only be used for cold applications, such as salad dressing. This is simply not true and has been thoroughly debunked in the scientific literature. High-quality, extra-virgin olive oil, which is full of antioxidants from the phenolic compounds, has been shown to have a smoke point of up to 420°F (215°C). I love the flavor that EVOO gives to green vegetables, and I use it every day in my own home cooking.

GHEE

Ghee hails from India and is a type of clarified butter that has been cooked long enough for the milk solids to lightly toast and infuse a rich, nutty flavor into the fat. Butter is not considered Paleo due to containing milk proteins, and proteins are frequently the component of food that causes an immune response. Ghee, however, has all milk proteins removed and is a type of "butter oil" that is Paleo friendly. It can be great to use in dishes where you would have used butter or as an alternative to EVOO or avocado oil for sautéing or roasting savory vegetables. There are many brands available that source from grass-fed cows, which is ideal. It has a long history of use in Ayurvedic medicine to support health.

LARD

When buying lard, avoid a hydrogenated version, typically sold in large plastic pails and which does not require refrigeration. It is typically bleached, deodorized and preserved with BHA and BHT, suspected carcinogens and hormone disruptors. Instead, choose freshly rendered lard in the refrigerated or frozen section, or look for jars in the grocery store aisles that say you must refrigerate after opening and have "pork fat" as the sole ingredient. Or, you can render it yourself at home from pork fat. I buy mine rendered and frozen from a local pasture-based farmer.

Mastering Stainless Steel Cookware

This book is written with instructions for stainless steel cookware. The Paleo lifestyle is more than just food; it includes making choices to avoid toxins in our homes and personal care products, and adopting healthy lifestyle habits like getting enough sleep, making time for play, appropriate exercise, etc. (I could write a whole book just on these healthy lifestyle factors.) But choosing nontoxic cookware is quite relevant to this book, and there is a reason why professional chefs and avid home cooks alike choose stainless steel cookware. It works incredibly well as long as you know how to use it properly.

For optimal results, stainless steel must be preheated before adding your cooking fat. The amount of time that a stainless steel pan needs to reach temperature will vary depending on the brand and construction, as well as on your stovetop.

On my glass-top electric stove, my pans need about 5 minutes at medium heat to get hot. You may only need 2 minutes. What's important is to test and learn your pans. It's also important never to heat a stainless steel pan over high heat because it will very quickly get far too hot and take a long time to cool down to an appropriate cooking temperature.

How do you test that your pan is hot enough? You'll need to use about ⅛ teaspoon of water and observe how it behaves when it hits the pan. When the pan is only slightly warm, the water will just pool and eventually simply evaporate. Once it's getting warmer, it will sizzle and sputter before evaporating. Don't make the mistake of thinking this means it is hot enough.

Wait 30 to 60 seconds and try again. What you want to see is for the drop of water to hold its shape as a single drop, almost like a ball of mercury, and scoot around the pan. For my fellow science nerds, this is due to the Leidenfrost effect, and it is why stainless steel can work so perfectly to sear meats and is actually an excellent non-stick cookware option.

Once your water drop holds its shape in the pan, you want to act quickly and add the oil, tilt and swirl the pan to coat the bottom, and then immediately start adding your food.

Now you can cook with non-stick confidence in your stainless steel cookware!

Side Dish Finder

This chart contains all the different vegetables and side dishes found throughout the book organized by how long they take to prepare.

You can use this chart to help you pair side dishes to go with your mains based on how many minutes they cook and which cooking method they use.

VEGETABLES	PREP TIME	COOK TIME	TOTAL TIME	COOKING METHOD	PAGE NUMBER
Garlicky Mustard Greens	5	5	10	stovetop	96
Sautéed Zucchini Coins with Basil	5	5	10	stovetop	93
Warm Lemon-Dill Cucumbers	3	7	10	stovetop	89
Steamed Broccoli	5	5–7	10–12	stovetop	22
Fried Ripe Plantains	3	6–10	<15	stovetop	62
Cauliflower Rice	5	10	15	bake @ 400°F (200°C)	53
Cheesy Creamed Spinach and Mushrooms	<5	10	15	stovetop	103
Ethiopian Cabbage	5	10	15	stovetop	100
Lemon-Garlic Brussels Sprout Chips	5	8–10	15	bake @ 350°F (180°C)	99
Nutty Coleslaw	15	0	15	no cook	25
Sautéed Radishes with Greens	5	10	15	stovetop	94
Spiced Beet Greens	5	7	15	stovetop	104
Zesty Mojo Red Cabbage Coleslaw	15	0	15	no cook	90
Smoky Roasted Asparagus	<5	10–15	15–20	bake @ 400°F (200°C)	97
Plantain Tortillas	5	12	<20	bake @ 375°F (190°C)	26
Colcannon	10	15	25	stovetop	107

VEGETABLES	PREP TIME	COOK TIME	TOTAL TIME	COOKING METHOD	PAGE NUMBER
Irish Carrot Parsnip Mash	5	20	25	stovetop	111
Roasted Mushrooms with Gremolata	10	12	25	bake @ 400°F (200°C)	108
Sautéed Kale or Collards with Tahini Sauce	10	15	25	stovetop	112
Crispy Roasted Brussels Sprouts with White BBQ Sauce	10	15–20	30	bake @ 425°F (220°C)	115
Crispy Baked Rosemary Garlic Steak Fries	5	25	30	bake @ 425°F (220°C)	120
Golden Roasted Cauliflower	10	20	30	bake @ 425°F (220°C)	119
Portobello Buns	10	20	30	bake @ 425°F (220°C)	57
Roasted Carrot Fries with Carrot Top Chimichurri	10	20	30	bake @ 400°F (200°C)	116
Sweet Potato Buns	10	20	30	bake @ 425°F (220°C)	66
Crispy Broccoli	5	25–30	30–35	bake @ 425°F (220°C)	41
Herbed Beet and Turnip Wedges	10	25	35	bake @ 425°F (220°C)	123
Spaghetti Squash Noodles	5	30	35	bake @ 425°F (220°C)	73
Cabbage Steaks	5	35–40	40–45	bake @ 425°F (220°C)	37

Batch Cooking Baking Guide

Are you a fan of batch cooking? Use this chart to see which dishes can be cooked together in the oven at the same temperature and for the same amount of time.

	BAKE TIME (MINUTES)	PAGE NUMBER
OVEN TEMP 350°F (180°C)		
Lemon-Garlic Brussels Sprout Chips	8–10	99
Flourless Chocolate Chip Cookies	12	147
Baked Spiced Pears with Honey	25	144
OVEN TEMP 375°F (190°C)		
Plantain Tortillas	12	26
Caribbean Cottage Pie	15	70
BBQ Chicken Pizza with Plantain Crust	30	33
OVEN TEMP 400°F (200°C)		
Persian Herb Frittata (Kuku Sabzi)	7	17
Cauliflower Rice	10	53
Lemon-Garlic Cod	10–12	77
Roasted Mushrooms with Gremolata	10–12	108
Smoky Roasted Asparagus	10–15	97
Roasted Carrot Fries with Carrot Top Chimichurri	15–20	116
Kickin' Salmon Patties with Comeback Sauce	20	79
Mozzarella Meatza	22–25	65
Bacon-Wrapped Mini Meatloaves with Carolina Mustard BBQ Sauce	25	69
Perfectly Crispy Chicken Thighs with Mushrooms and Honey Mustard	15–20	35

	BAKE TIME (MINUTES)	PAGE NUMBER
OVEN TEMP 425°F (220°C)		
Coconut Shrimp with Orange Dipping Sauce	10	81
Crispy Roasted Brussels Sprouts with White BBQ Sauce	15–20	115
Easy No-Breading Chicken Parmesan	12–15	30
Golden Roasted Cauliflower	20	119
Portobello Buns	20	57
Sweet Potato Buns	20	66
Crispy Baked Rosemary Garlic Steak Fries	22–25	120
Crispy Broccoli	25–30	41
Herbed Beet and Turnip Wedges	22–25	123
Baked BBQ Chicken Thighs Three Ways	30	38
Sheet Pan Chicken and Crispy Broccoli	30	41
Spaghetti Squash Noodles	30	73
Crispy Brazilian Chicken Wings with Avocado Crema	35–40	42
Ranch Chicken Drumsticks with Cabbage Steaks	35–40	37

Partially Used Fresh Ingredients Guide

Food waste is a terrible thing, and to help prevent it in your home I have grouped together the recipes that utilize partial amounts of fresh ingredients so that you can see at a glance how to pair recipes in a given week to make sure that you use up all of any given fresh ingredient. Recipes that call for an entire unit of an ingredient (i.e., a full can of coconut milk) are not included in these lists.

 COCONUT MILK

One can of coconut milk typically contains 14 fl oz, or 414 ml, which is 1¾ cups. Depending on the brand, it is only good in the refrigerator for 2–4 days after opening, so to avoid having to throw out leftover coconut milk, plan to make a few recipes that use it close to one another.

One thing I like to do is default to just making Chia Pudding (page 139) when I have coconut milk leftover, scaling the recipe up or down depending on exactly how much I have. Another helpful option is to make a single or double batch of the Fresh Mozzarella (page 162) and freeze it to have ready to use later.

RECIPE	MEASUREMENT	PAGE NUMBER
Stovetop Creamy Tuna Casserole	2 tbsp (30 ml) (optional)	85
Mediterranean Herbed Lamb Burgers with Tzatziki Sauce	¼ cup (60 ml)	55
Avocado Crema	¼ cup (60 ml)	156
Ground Beef Stroganoff with Cauliflower Rice	¼ to ½ cup (60 to 120 ml)	53
Super Green Soup	½ cup (120 ml) (optional)	128
Fresh Mozzarella	½ cup (120 ml)	162
Cheesy Creamed Spinach and Mushrooms	¾ cup (180 ml)	103
Rich Dark Chocolate Chia Pudding	¾ cup (180 ml)	139
Zuppa Toscana	1 cup (240 ml) (optional)	133

 CELERY

What I like to do with any leftover celery is to slice it and freeze it raw, using it within about 3 or 4 months. To make it last longer in the freezer, you can blanch it for about 3 minutes in boiling water first, then freeze (I never do this, though). Another idea: stalks of celery + your favorite nut or seed butter on top makes a great snack for adults and kids alike, too.

RECIPE	MEASUREMENT	PAGE NUMBER
Beet Marinara	2 stalks	164
Stovetop Creamy Tuna Casserole	2 stalks	85
Super Green Soup	3–4 stalks	128
Roux-less Shrimp Creole	4 stalks	82

 FRESH GINGER

The easiest way to never waste fresh ginger again is to simply freeze it. It is actually much easier to grate using a zester when frozen. When buying fresh ginger, look for plump roots without any wrinkles that feel firm and are fragrant. Use frozen ginger within 6 months.

RECIPE	MEASUREMENT	PAGE NUMBER
Egg Drop Soup	1 tsp minced	127
Ethiopian Cabbage	2 tsp (10 g) minced	100
Mongolian Beef with Steamed Broccoli	1 tbsp (14 g) minced	61
Super Green Soup	1 tbsp (14 g) minced	128
Sautéed Kale or Collards with Tahini Sauce	1½ tbsp (21 g) minced	112
Sheet Pan Chicken and Crispy Broccoli	2 tbsp (28 g) minced	41

FRESH HERBS

My top tip for never wasting fresh herbs is to save them all and use them in a Persian Herb Frittata (Kuku Sabzi) (page 17). The recipe is very forgiving and you can adjust the herb/green ratio significantly and still come up with a delicious dish.

 CILANTRO

RECIPE	MEASUREMENT	PAGE NUMBER
Mojo Shrimp Skillet with Cauliflower Rice	garnish	80
BBQ Chicken Pizza with Plantain Crust	garnish	33
Mediterranean-Herbed Lamb Burgers with Tzatziki Sauce	2 tbsp (2 g) chopped	55
Zesty Mojo Red Cabbage Coleslaw	½ packed cup (10 g)	90
Caribbean Cottage Pie	½ bunch	70
Fire-Roasted Salsa Soup with Chicken	½ bunch for garnish	131
Super Green Soup	½ bunch	128
Guacamole-Stuffed Chicken Poppers	1 packed cup (20 g)	29
Shortcut Fire-Roasted Salsa	1 packed cup (20 g)	157

 PARSLEY

RECIPE	MEASUREMENT	PAGE NUMBER
Ground Beef Stroganoff with Cauliflower Rice	garnish	53
Irish Carrot Parsnip Mash	chopped for garnish	111
Chicken Caulifredo with Steamed Broccoli	garnish	22
Roasted Mushrooms with Gremolata	2 tbsp (8 g) chopped	108
Bacon-Wrapped Mini Meatloaves with Carolina Mustard BBQ Sauce	⅓ cup (18 g)	69

 DILL

RECIPE	MEASUREMENT	PAGE NUMBER
Mediterranean-Herbed Lamb Burgers with Tzatziki Sauce	2–4 tbsp (7–14 g) chopped	55
Warm Lemon-Dill Cucumbers	1 tbsp (4 g) chopped	89
Persian Herb Frittata (Kuku Sabzi)	½ cup (26 g) chopped	17

Acknowledgments

To my husband Andy, #1 recipe tester: Thank you for your unwavering support and enthusiasm for all that I do. This book wouldn't have been possible without you, your feedback and all of those grocery store runs you made for me while I was busy cooking and writing.

To Jean Choi: Thank you for the beautiful photographs! I have admired your work for years, and I consider myself so lucky that you brought my recipes to life with your photos in this book. I can't thank you enough for the incredible work.

To my readers: Thank you for all of the feedback about the kinds of recipes that would help you most and for being so excited to always learn from me and try my recipes. It is an honor to be a part of your healing journey.

To my fellow authors and writers: Thank you for being so supportive of my first book and the recipes on my website. You know who you are. A rising tide lifts all ships, and I am lucky to have so many friends in the community.

To Page Street Publishing: For working with me to bring another labor of love into the world. I am so grateful!

About the Author

Amanda Torres, a neuroscientist by training, is passionate about sharing good food and science-backed lifestyle information to inspire and empower others to reclaim good health. She is always sharing new recipes and educational articles on her website TheCuriousCoconut.com, a trusted resource since 2012. She is also the author of the bestselling cookbook *Latin American Paleo Cooking*.

She experienced the healing power of food firsthand when she first went Paleo in 2010, after failing to lose weight following conventional advice and facing extremely poor health and a long list of scary health problems. By the end of year one on the Paleo diet, she had lost 80 pounds and reversed pre-diabetes, hypertension, metabolic syndrome, rosacea, dyslipidemia and depression. This lifestyle has also kept her autoimmune skin condition, hidradenitis suppurativa, mostly in complete remission. She has maintained her weight loss and good health to date.

Amanda also loves sharing information about mindfulness, meditation, Chinese medicine, acupuncture and yoga with her audience, since she has found these tried-and-true ancient tools to be the key to a well-rounded healthy lifestyle in our hectic and out-of-balance modern world. Her website is also a great place to learn more about nontoxic living and safer skincare products and cosmetics. Both food and lifestyle can be either medicine or poison, and Amanda is passionate about helping others find their medicine.

She is the fine-art photographer for the design and publishing company Mobius Theory, which she co-owns with her husband Andy.

Index